THE MACROECONOMICS OF OPEN ECONOMIES UNDER LABOUR MOBILITY

To the people who migrate in the quest for a better life and for Ρανια, Μυρωνα, Ελευθερια and Αννα–Χρυσανθη

The Macroeconomics of Open Economies under Labour Mobility

GEORGE M. AGIOMIRGIANAKIS
University of Hull, United Kingdom;
City University, London, United Kingdom
and CNR, Italy

Ashgate

Aldershot • Brookfield USA • Singapore • Sydney

© George M. Agiomirgianakis 1999

Published by
Ashgate Publishing Ltd
Gower House
Croft Road
Aldershot
Hants GU11 3HR
England

Ashgate Publishing Company
Old Post Road
Brookfield
Vermont 05036
USA

Ashgate website: http://www.ashgate.com

British Library Cataloguing in Publication Data
Agiomirgianakis, George M.
  The macroeconomics of open economies under labour mobility
  1. Labour mobility 2. Labour mobility - Government policy
  3. Labour economics
  I. Title
  331.1'27

Library of Congress Catalog Card Number: 99-72843

ISBN 1 84014 949 3

Printed in Great Britain by
Antony Rowe Ltd, Chippenham, Wiltshire

Contents

v

List of Figures

List of Tables

Acknowledgements

During the time of this research I have benefited from the help of several people who, at various stages, became familiar with aspects of my work.

Special thanks go to Athina Zervoyianni for extensive suggestions and encouragement throughout this research. I would also like to thank Emmanuel Pikoulakis and George Alogoskoufis who made valuable comments and suggestions that affected considerably the direction of this research. I am also thankful to Emmanuel Petrakis, Tapan Biswas, Geoffrey Wood, Michael Ryan, and Gerry Makepeace for providing helpful comments on various chapters.

The author and the publisher are grateful to the following for permission to reproduce extracts from: *The Journal of Macroeconomics*, Vol. 20, No. 2, Spring 1998; *The International Journal of Finance and Economics*, Vol. 1, April 1996; *Business and Economics for the 21st Century*, Vol. 1, 1997, by permission of the Business and Economics Society International; *The Journal of Economic Integration*, Vol. 14, No. 1, March 1999 and *The Economic Record*, Vol. 61, December 1991.

Introduction

International labour mobility is an issue of increasing interest and importance to international economics for many reasons. First, international labour flows affect the size, the age structure and the skills of the labour force in both the country of the origin and the host country. Second, the magnitude of human flows across countries has become relatively large over the last few years: in the early 1990s some 100 million people were resident outside their nations of citizenship (see Widgren, 1987; Russell and Teitelbaum, 1992). Third, the scale of international labour flows is expected to rise in the future as a result of widening economic differentials, of demographic pressures, of differential labour-force growth rates and of the extension of transportation and communications. Moreover, many governments of countries where labour is in abundance are currently following policies which either explicitly or implicitly promote exports of labour.[1] Given the high level of unemployment in many western countries, the expected growth of labour inflows generates concerns by both policy-makers and the general public about the possible adverse effects of immigration on the employment of native workers (see Djajic, 1985; Brecher and Choudhri, 1987; Burda and Wyplosz, 1992; De New and Zimmermann, 1993a and b; Freeman, 1993). Fourth, migration flows are increasingly volatile and unpredictable, with political as well as economic causes and consequences (see Russell and Teitelbaum, 1992). Indeed, recent political and economic changes in Europe have resulted in millions of international migrants from Eastern European countries to European Union countries (see Salt, 1992; Okolski, 1992; Burda, 1993). At the same time, countries of Central and Eastern Europe, such as Poland, are experiencing inflows of foreign workers from Russia, Lithuania and Ukraine (see *New York Times*, 6 October 1991). Also, traditionally emigration countries, such as Italy, Greece, Spain and Portugal, not only have become net immigration countries but, along with Germany, are also the main destination countries in Europe (see Chesnais, 1992; Salt, 1992; Faini and Venturini, 1993). Fifth, the financial flows associated with international labour movements are substantial: official remittances were nearly US$66 billion in 1989, second in value only to trade in crude oil and larger than official development assistance (see Russell

1

and Teitelbaum, 1992). Finally, the issue of international labour mobility becomes more important when we take into account the fact that labour flows and the resulting economic flows are concentrated in a few world regions, namely the sub-Saharan Africa, Western Europe, North America, Australia and the oil-rich states of the Arab Gulf.

In Western Europe, in a time of growing unification and harmonisation of nations in European Union, the issue of 'foreign labour' and its consequences is an issue of growing significance. Because in the postwar period many Western European countries responded to general labour shortages by allowing or promoting substantial labour inflows from the less-developed countries, the stock of foreign nationals in the European Community in 1989 was accounted for approximately four per cent of the resident population in member states or some 13 million: EC-foreigners accounted for 1.5 per cent and non-EC foreigners accounted for 2.5 per cent. There are differences, however, between the member states regarding the percentage of foreign labour in their national population. As Winkelmann and Zimmermann (1992) report, in 1989 the share of 'foreign workers', i.e. non-EC workers, in the total population of European countries was 15.7 per cent in Luxembourg, 2.6 per cent in Germany, 2.1 per cent in France, 1.9 per cent in Belgium, 1.4 per cent in the United Kingdom, 1.2 per cent in the Netherlands and 0.9 per cent in Denmark. Of particular importance, is also the share of foreign employment in the national employment of member states: 33.2 per cent in Luxembourg, 7.7 per cent in Germany, 6.4 per cent in France and Belgium, 4.2 per cent in the United Kingdom, 3.1 per cent in the Netherlands, 1.4 per cent in Denmark and 0.9 per cent in Greece. Also a number of EC nationals work in another member country other than their native: Winkelmann and Zimmermann (1992) and Salt (1992) report that two million workers come from within the current member states representing 40 per cent of foreign workers in EC. The establishment of a unified labour market among the 12 member states of the European Community is expected to increase labour mobility further within the Community from member states with high labour force growth, such as Ireland, to the member states with a low labour force growth, such as Denmark (see Johnson and Zimmerman, 1992). Also, given the established positive rather than negative relation between international trade and international labour mobility (see Molle and Van Mourik, 1988) the increasing trend in trade between the member states in the European Community is expected to encourage the free movement of labour. On the other hand, recent political and economic changes in Eastern Europe have raised the possibility of a resumption of mass migration towards the West (see Faini and Venturini, 1993; Straubhaar and Zimmermann, 1992).

These stylised facts imply that international labour mobility is an issue of increasing importance in today's economies and thus in international economics. Indeed, in recent years there has been an expansion of the already vast literature on international labour mobility (ILM). This literature is characterised by a variety of research interests, reflecting the different aspects of international labour mobility. As Molle and Van Mourik (1988) note, existing studies of ILM could be classified into three main groups (although, in many cases, these groups overlap between themselves): a) microeconomic studies; b) studies concerned with the welfare aspects of ILM; and c) 'aggregate models'.

Microeconomic studies focus on the theoretical aspects of ILM from the individual migrant's point of view. In these studies the decision to migrate is assumed to result from the behaviour of a utility maximiser consumer-worker who faces the option to work in his native country or to work abroad (see, for example, Djajic, 1989; Stark, 1991; Hill, 1987; Raffelhuschen, 1992).

The bulk of the literature on ILM is concerned with the welfare effects of migration from the point of view of both the host and sending countries, that is, the issue of whether international mobility of labour will depress the wages of the host country or whether there will be some benefit for the sending country (see, for example, Greenwood, 1969; Djajic, 1985; Simon, 1989; Rivera-Batiz, 1989; Quibria, 1989; Brecher and Choudhri, 1987, 1990; Abowd and Freeman, 1991; Borjas, 1991, 1992; Nikas, 1992; Clarke, 1993; Ichino, 1993; De New and Zimmermann, 1993a and b; Freeman, 1993).

'Aggregate models' focus on issues like the *spatial aspects* of ILM; the *sectoral employment patterns* of foreign workers; the *time patterns* of foreign-worker employment; and the economic behaviour of the migrants in the host country (see, for example, Greenwood, 1969, 1986; Molle and Van Mourik, 1988; Kumcu, 1989; Abowd and Freeman, 1991; Stark, 1991; Winkelmann and Zimmerman, 1992; Vijverberg, 1993; Faini and Venturini, 1993). These models are often 'gravity type models' in which the size of international labour flows is determined by a combination of social and economic variables in both the country of origin and the host country. These variables are further classified as push factors in the sending country, such as the growth of the labour force, pull factors in the host country, such as labour shortage, resistance factors including the cost of movement, and stimulus factors, such as differences in wages.

While some studies, also take into account other factors, such as information costs, uncertainty, lifetime income, asymmetry in information and the variety of population, much of this literature attributes the movement of labour to international difference in the standards of living,[2] including real wages differentials.[3] Indeed, a common assumption of the existing ILM literature is that wage differentials between countries generate international labour mobility. This assumption can be traced back to Hicks (1932), who notes that '... differences in net economic advantages, chiefly differences in wages, are the main causes of migration ...'.

Although international labour mobility has been examined extensively from the international-trade or microeconomic point of view, it has been very little analysed in the context of a macroeconomic framework. Indeed, in today's world of open economies where international labour flows are large, increasing and most importantly volatile, most of the studies on international macroeconomics are carried out under the assumption of no international labour mobility. Yet analysing the macroeconomic implications of international labour mobility is a worthwhile exercise: in the last few years it has been generally recognised that the behaviour of labour markets is crucial to macroeconomic performance. Thus factors like international labour mobility, which affects the stock, the age structure and the skills of a country's labour force, will eventually affect the productive capacity of the economy and hence its overall performance. Indeed, two questions arise: how are the macrovariables affected by ILM and what are its economic policy implications?

Moreover, because the micro-literature on international labour mobility borrows assumptions and methodology from the literature on internal labour mobility, a key element of international labour mobility is lost, namely that labour is moving away from countries with a relatively weaker currency towards countries with a relatively stronger currency. This implies that the real exchange rate is important in understanding international labour flows. Okolski (1992), for example, notes that '... greatly overvalued Western currencies and the enormously high purchasing power at home of wages earned in the EC countries by migrant workers from the Central and Eastern Europe were important stimuli to taking up temporary employment abroad ...'. Indeed, while in internal labour mobility nominal-wage differentials may be the main reason for moving from one job to another, in international labour mobility the decision to work abroad is usually based on the real-consumption-wage differential between the home and the rest of the world which takes account of differences in the cost of living. Quoting again Okolski '... the standard of living is much lower in Central and Eastern Europe than in the West. This is why many people from the countries of Central and Eastern Europe, in an attempt to improve their well-being, emigrate westwards'. Yet, in a world of flexible exchange rates, real consumption-wage differentials vary according to real-exchange rate variability, in contrast to the case of a fixed real exchange rate between home and abroad, assumed often in many microeconomic studies.

In addition, macroeconomic policies in one country, by affecting the push and pull factors of ILM and thus generating international labour flows, can transmit disturbances to other countries (see, for example, Ghosh, 1992). Indeed, in the last few years, researchers and policy-makers in Europe have emphasised the need for inter-government cooperation in tackling the problem of international labour movements (see Chesnais, 1992; Salt, 1992; Okolski, 1992).

Finally, international labour mobility through its effect on domestic unemployment, may affect both the process of wage-setting and the economic policy in a country. The aim of this book is to extend the theoretical literature on open economy macroeconomics by exploring the role of international labour mobility in the behaviour of open economies with flexible exchange rates. In particular, the book attempts to address five main issues: a) the implications of ILM for national monetary autonomy; b) the consequences of international migration for the transmission of disturbances across countries; c) the nature of interactions between ILM and capital accumulation; d) the impact of international migration on wage-setting in unionised economies; and e) how international migration affects the outcomes of macroeconomic policy games between trade unions and policy-makers.

In chapter 1 we incorporate the possibility of international labour mobility into a dynamic macro model of a small open economy with a flexible exchange rate and a competitive labour market and explore its role in the adjustment of this economy to unanticipated monetary policy changes. While the bulk of the literature on exchange-rate dynamics postulates perfect capital mobility, most studies make the assumption of no international mobility of labour (see, for example, Dornbush, 1976; Sachs, 1980; Ahtiala, 1989; Devereux and Purvis, 1990. Chapter 1 can be viewed as an attempt to extend this literature by taking account of the possibility of international labour mobility. Indeed, two issues are addressed: first, what are the macroeconomic implications of monetary expansions under ILM; second, how the presence of ILM affects exchange-rate variability following unanticipated monetary shocks.

International labour mobility in chapter 1 is assumed to result from the behaviour of a utility maximiser consumer-worker (C-W) who has two options as far as employment is concerned: to work in his native country or to work abroad. The two types of work are taken to be imperfect substitutes due to differences in work-satisfaction arising from work time. In this framework, if domestic residents are utility maximisers and have the option to 'work home' or 'work abroad', the domestic labour supply is sensitive to changes in both the domestic wage rate and the foreign wage rate in domestic consumer-price units. This gives rise to an additional role for the nominal exchange rate: changes in the nominal exchange rate affect workers' choices both indirectly, through their impact on the domestic real consumption wage via the consumer price index (CPI), and, directly, by making domestic nominal wages more/ less attractive relative to foreign wages in domestic-currency units. Therefore, changes in monetary policy will influence both the direction and the volume of international flows of labour.

Our analysis shows that an unanticipated domestic monetary expansion, by causing a real exchange rate depreciation, will on impact cause a fall in the domestic labour supply both because it will decrease the home real consumption wage and because it will increase the foreign real wage in domestic currency purchasing power units. That is, domestic workers will reduce their total supply of labour and will also undertake more work abroad. This will cause a large fall in domestic employment and thus a large short-run drop in domestic output. This has a straightforward policy implication: as national labour markets become more integrated, any attempt by the government of a single country to surprise the public with an unanticipated monetary expansion will have a larger negative short-run impact on domestic economic activity. However, unlike capital mobility, labour mobility is found to have no unambiguous effect on exchange-rate variability: the short-run response of the nominal exchange rate to an unanticipated expansionary monetary policy may or may not be larger with ILM.

In chapter 2 we explore the role of international migration of labour in the transmission of fiscal disturbances between countries. This chapter extends our analysis in chapter 1 in three directions. First, it considers a world of two interdependent, symmetric economies. Second, it assumes that both economies operate under conditions of international migration of labour (IML) which we distinguish from international labour mobility (ILM) in that the former is a continuous process through time while the latter involves instantaneous adjustment. Third, we consider a fiscal contraction originated abroad and investigate the role of IML in the transmission of this disturbance to the home economy.

Much of the research on the international transmission of fiscal policies is carried out under the assumption of no international migration (see, for example, Allen and Kennen, 1980; Mundell, 1983; Argy and Salop, 1983; Oudiz and Sachs, 1984; McKibbin and Sachs, 1986; Jensen, 1991; Van der Ploeg, 1988, 1995). This research either assumes that labour supply is a negative function of the real exchange rate because workers are concerned with the real purchasing power of their wages, or that labour supply is independent of the real exchange rate and nominal wage rigidity prevails in the labour market. In models where labour supply is assumed to be a negative function of the real exchange rate, each country's employment and output supply are also negative functions of the real exchange rate and fiscal expansions in one country are negatively transmitted abroad. A fiscal expansion at home, for example, by appreciating the real exchange rate, will lead to higher home employment and output at the expense of lower foreign employment and output. Thus, fiscal expansions in one country are beggar-thy-neighbour policies. In models where labour supply is independent of the real exchange rate and nominal wage rigidity prevails in the labour markets as in a Mundell-Fleming world, the supply of domestic output is a positive function of the prices of domestic goods. In this case, a fiscal expansion in one country raises the price level both at home and abroad and thus, by reducing real product wages, raises output supply in the foreign economy as well as in the domestic economy.

To incorporate international migration into a two-country framework, we follow the literature on labour migration in assuming that international migration is generated by real consumption-wage differentials between the two countries; that migration is a continuous process taking place over time; that at any point in time, labour supply in each country is fixed by the past decisions of workers about migration; and that each country's workforce is fully employed.

With a fixed labour supply in the short run and without nominal rigidities, an unanticipated foreign fiscal contraction leads to a real exchange rate appreciation but has no impact on employment and output at home and abroad. Over time, however, the appreciation of the real exchange rate, by lowering the foreign real consumption wage relative to the home real consumption wage, generates a net flow of labour from the foreign economy towards the home economy. As a result, each country's labour force changes: the home economy experiences an increase in its workforce at the expense of the foreign economy. Under conditions of full employment, this leads to an increase in home output and a drop in foreign output. Thus, our analysis shows that fiscal disturbances originated in one country will be transmitted over time to other countries through international labour migration. Our analysis also shows that international migration will eliminate any real-consumption-wage differentials created by unanticipated foreign fiscal contractions; and that the higher is the degree of IML, the shorter will be the period during which real wage differentials between the two countries persist. By contrast, without IML and nominal rigidities, labour supply in each country will be fixed both in the short run and over time and thus an unanticipated foreign fiscal contraction will have no effect on home output. Moreover, our analysis shows that the variability of the real exchange rate will be larger in the absence of IML than in the presence of IML.

In chapter 3 we extend the analysis in chapter 1 by allowing for changes over time in the capital stock and by considering the effects of unanticipated nonmonetary shocks.

We start by first discussing our assumptions about the production side of the economy. As in the previous chapters, the domestic economy is assumed to produce a single good. However, here this single good is not only output available for consumption but also an input for gross capital formation. Also, much of the literature on gross capital formation assumes that labour supply is inelastic. Since our focus is on the macroeconomic effects of international labour mobility (ILM), in this chapter we relax the assumption of an inelastic labour supply in favour of a labour supply depending upon the domestic real wage and foreign real wage. Next we present the macroeconomic model and examine the adjustment of the domestic economy in response to an exogenous increase in the demand for real bonds and for domestic output. We proceed to the analysis of this model in two steps. First, we assume static expectations. This allows us to gain some insights into the short-run effects of the two shocks on domestic output. Then, rational expectations are assumed and changes over time in the capital stock and the stock of real bonds are considered. The role of ILM in the impact, dynamic and long-run effects of the two shocks is investigated.

Our analysis shows that an unanticipated increase in the demand for real bonds leads to results similar to those obtained in the case of the monetary expansion analysed in chapter 1. Our findings regarding the effects of the aggregate demand shock are in line with the literature on capital formation: like in, for example, Tobin and Buiter (1976), Pikoulakis (1984) and Murphy (1989), we find that an unanticipated increase in the demand for domestic output will on impact cause a real exchange rate appreciation and that, by 'crowding-out' investment, will lead to a reduction in the steady-state stock of capital.

The main difference between our model and those of the existing literature on capital accumulation lies in our assumption about labour supply: most of the literature on capital formation assumes that labour is supplied inelastically. In our model we adopt the more general assumption that labour supply depends on both the real domestic wage and the real foreign wage in terms of domestic-currency purchasing power units, through international labour mobility.

Although the presence of ILM does not affect the long-run properties of the model, it affects the size of the impact effects, as well as the dynamic adjustment of the economy in response to the two unanticipated shocks. In particular, our analysis shows that the presence of ILM is associated with three effects: 'an employment effect', 'an output effect' and 'a real exchange rate effect'. That is, the presence of ILM, by increasing the sensitivity of labour supply to changes in the real exchange rate, will increase the sensitivity of domestic employment and domestic output to changes in the real exchange rate, induced by the two unanticipated shocks. In the context of our model where capital is not mobile internationally, our findings suggest that the presence of ILM reduces the variability of the real exchange rate following each shock. Finally, the presence of ILM affects, through the above effects, both the accumulation of capital and the accumulation of real bonds.

In chapters 1–3 we ignore imperfections in the labour market by assuming a competitive labour market. However, the labour markets of most countries do not conform with this assumption: most western countries are currently experiencing a persistently high level of unemployment; and changes in the marginal revenue product of labour are usually accompanied by changes in the level of employment rather than in real wages. These stylised facts of today's economies, namely unemployment and real wage rigidity, should in principle be taken into account in examining the macroeconomic implications of international migration of labour.

Contemporary economic theory suggests three approaches to unemployment and rigid wages that differ from the traditional consideration of minimum wage legislation. The first is the 'implicit contracts' theory which assumes that firms supply their workers with insurance against income uncertainty. This results in a relatively stable real wage. The second is the 'trade union' model which is based on the assumption that trade unions have some bargaining power over wages and/or employment. The third approach is the 'efficiency wages' theory which assumes that labour effort is related to real wages offered by firms.

In chapter 4 we incorporate the possibility of IML into a trade-union model of a small open economy with a flexible exchange rate. Our choice in this chapter of a trade-union approach rather than an efficiency-wage approach is based on two considerations. First, as Nickell (1990) notes '... we have some evidence in favour of the efficiency wage story but it is not, as yet, overwhelming ...'. Second, trade unions play a decisive role in wage-employment decisions in many industrial countries, particularly in Europe.

We restrict our analysis to the case of a small open economy which faces outflows of labour (emigration). We also assume that the economy is made up of many identical firms, all unionised. This assumption allows us to consider the wage-employment bargaining within an individual firm as a microcosm of the entire labour market wage-employment bargaining. Throughout chapter 4 we assume that the union is concerned only with the welfare of its existing members and wishes to maximise the expected utility of its median member.

We start by presenting the efficient bargains model of trade unions in the closed-economy case. In the efficient bargains model, the union and the firm bargain over the joint determination of the wage rate and the level of employment. The outcome of this bargaining is Pareto efficient, that is, it lies on the contract curve. Then, we extend the efficient bargains model to the open-economy case. Finally, we open up the economy to international migration.

The decision to migrate is assumed to be based on an existing wage differential between the small open economy and the rest of the world. In this context, migration outflows reduce the membership of the trade union in the domestic country. Since the union is concerned with the welfare of its existing members, lower membership results in higher wages as there are fewer union jobs to be protected. Hence employment and union membership remain lower after the migration flows have ceased and unemployment may be lower or unchanged depending on whether or not 'outsiders' are migrating. We also show that through international migration the home real consumer wage is positively related to the rest-of-the-world wage and negatively related to average migration cost: an increase in the rest-of-the-world wage or a decrease in the migration cost will induce a larger proportion of insiders to migrate abroad. Therefore, the smaller number of remaining insiders, acting through their union, will succeed in achieving higher real consumer wages at home. On the other hand, an increase in the real exchange rate will increase the home real product wage. However, the sign of the change in the home real consumer wage is ambiguous. Finally, a positive technological shock, by strengthening the bargaining position of the trade union, is shown to lead to an increase in both the real consumer wage and the employment level.

While in chapter 4 we examine the effects of international migration in the context of an efficient-bargains trade-union model where a representative union and a firm are bargaining over the joint determination of the wage rate and the level of employment, we ignore the role of governments by implicitly assuming that either they play a passive role or policy variables remain unchanged. Obviously, governments do not play a passive role: they have their own objectives with respect to unemployment and inflation and these objectives are affected by trade unions' choices. Indeed, trade union behaviour often motivates government actions. Similarly, government actions affect the unions' objectives. Rational trade-union behaviour thus implies that government actions have to be taken into account. Within this framework of actions and counteractions by trade unions and the government, economic policy and wage formation must be analysed as a two-player game.

In chapter 5 we incorporate the possibility of international migration into a simple macroeconomic-policy game between governments and trade unions. The game-theoretic approach to macroeconomic policy in open economies has been expanding rapidly in recent years: see Rogoff (1985), Gylfanson and Lindbeck (1986, 1991), Canzoneri and Henderson (1988), Driffill and Schultz (1992), Zervoyianni (1993) and Jensen (1993a and b). However, macroeconomic-policy games have been analysed within the context of models in which the labour force is taken to be fixed. In the model we present and analyse in chapter 5 we distinguish between the initial labour force which is given exogenously and the effective labour force which depends on the rate of labour migration. Like in the previous chapters, international migration is assumed to be generated by an existing real-consumption-wage differential between the home country and the rest of the world. Because real consumption wages depend on nominal wages and on nominal money supplies, the size of migration flows and thus the size of the effective labour force also depends on the actions of the two players, i.e. the union and the government. Since changes in the effective labour force will affect unemployment levels, they will also affect the objectives of both players. In effect, the presence of international migration implies additional interactions between the two players.

We start by considering a small open economy that takes all foreign variables as given. The entire domestic labour force in this economy is assumed to be organised in a single all embracing monopoly union which sets nominal wages unilaterally with a view to maximising a utility function defined in terms of real consumption wages and employment. Wage contracts are assumed to be for one period: at the end of each period, unions and firms are assumed to sign contracts that specify nominal wages and employment rules for the following period. On the other hand, policy-makers set the money supply at the beginning of each period with a view to maximising a macro welfare function defined over home employment and consumer price index (CPI) inflation. Both a non-cooperative and a cooperative game between the union and the policy-makers are considered, first in the case of no migration and then under conditions of international migration.

Under no migration, a non-cooperative regime is shown to lead to relatively high real wages and a non-zero rate of inflation. A cooperative regime leads to a relatively low level of unemployment and zero rate of CPI inflation. As a result, policy-makers are better off under cooperation. On the other hand, the trade union is shown to be better off under the non-cooperative regime.

International migration does not affect the relative desirability of each regime from the point of view of the two players. However, it does improve the absolute position of each player in each regime and thus it constitutes a Pareto improvement relative to the non-migration situation. The reason is that by affecting domestic unemployment through its impact on the domestic effective labour force and by having no effect on CPI inflation, international migration creates a positive externality for both players and thus it improves their welfare.

Next we extend our analysis to the case of two interdependent economies. Because in an interdependent world policies in one country affect macroeconomic aggregates in other countries, national policy-makers are engaged in a strategic interplay. Following, for example, Rogoff (1985), Canzoneri and Henderson (1988), Zervoyianni (1993) and Jensen (1993a and b), we consider two regimes for the policy-makers: they may behave as non-cooperative players or they may cooperate. On the other hand, we assume that unions cooperate neither between themselves nor with the policy makers.

The analysis shows that Rogoff's (1985) conclusion that monetary policies are more expansionary when policy-makers cooperate than when they do not cooperate does not necessarily hold under conditions of international migration. The reason is that in a non-cooperative regime, the presence of international migration allows each policy-maker to exercise an additional positive influence on his country's unemployment by increasing the money supply: an increase in the money supply of a country relative to the money supply abroad, lowers the effective labour force of the country where the monetary expansion occurs by inducing migration flows through its impact on the real wage differentials. In a non-cooperative regime, each policy maker will therefore choose a relatively more expansionary monetary policy. In a cooperative regime, on the other hand, each policy-maker knows that any attempt to induce a drop in his country's effective labour force through migration flows will be offset by equal attempts abroad. As a result, each policy-maker's incentive to use monetary policy to reduce unemployment is relatively weaker. Accordingly, whether monetary policies will be more expansionary under cooperation than under non-cooperation depends upon the relative size of two opposing externalities: the negative externality arising from the real-exchange-rate effect on CPIs of unilateral monetary expansions; and the positive externality arising from the impact of these expansions on the effective labour force through international migration. If the welfare effect of the positive externality dominates, then cooperation between home and foreign policy-makers will lead to a Pareto improvement relative to a non-cooperative regime and inter-government cooperation in the monetary field will turn out to be advantageous.

Notes

1   Such policies are followed, for example, by Turkey, Mexico, India, Albania, South Korea, the Philippines, Cuba, Jamaica, Barbados, Pakistan, Sri Lanka and Nicaragua.
2   The dependence of international labour mobility on differences in the standards of living between countries may rise the issue of whether the standards of living converge. In a study by Evans and Karras (1993), it is shown that the hypothesis of convergence in standards of living, implied by the neoclassical growth models, can be rejected across countries except among a sample of rich countries. Therefore, other things being equal, international differences in standards of living should be expected to increase the incentives favouring the international movement of people.
3   See, for example, various papers in the May 1983 special issue of the *Journal of International Economics* on international factor mobility, as well as, Rodriguez, 1976; Djajic, 1985; 1987; Greenwood and McDowell, 1986; Stark, 1991b; Straubhaar and Zimmermann, 1992; Burda , 1993.

1 International Mobility of Labour and Monetary Policy in a Small Open Economy

1 Introduction

Most of the existing literature on international labour mobility (ILM) deals with either the causes of labour mobility or the 'welfare effects' of labour mobility, that is, the question of whether international mobility of labour will depress the wages of the host country or whether there will be some benefit for the sending country (see, for example, Greenwood, 1969; Djajic, 1985; Rivera-Batiz, 1989; Quibria, 1989; Brecher and Choudhri, 1987, 1990; Abowd and Freeman, 1991; Borjas and Freeman, 1992; Nikas, 1992; Ichino, 1993; De New and Zimmerman, 1993a and b; Freeman,1993). This literature often relies on ad hoc assumptions regarding the workers motives for moving from one job to another: authors either incorporate in their analysis several social and economic variables (gravity models) (see e.g. Greenwood, 1969; Stark, 1991; Abowd and Freeman, 1991; Zimmermann, 1992; Faini and Venturini, 1993; Vijverberg, 1993) or employ models which are based on the assumption that labour mobility depends upon expected real income differences (see e.g. Rodriguez, 1976; Djajic, 1989; Borjas, 1991; Stark, 1991; Burda and Wyplosz, 1992, 1993; Baldwin and Venables, 1993; Dolado, 1993). Moreover, none of these studies has incorporated the possibility of international labour mobility into a macroeconomic framework.

The purpose of this chapter is to incorporate the possibility of international labour mobility into a macro model of a small open economy with a flexible exchange rate and a competitive labour market and explore its role in the adjustment of the economy to monetary-policy changes. While the bulk of the literature on exchange rate dynamics assumes capital mobility, most studies make the assumption of no international mobility of labour (see e.g. Dornbush, 1976; Sachs, 1980; Driskill and McCafferty, 1987; Ahtiala, 1989; Devereux and Purvis, 1990). This chapter can be viewed as an attempt to extend the

14

international macroeconomics literature by taking account of the possibility of international labour mobility. Indeed, two issues are addressed: first, what are the macroeconomic implications of monetary expansions under ILM; and, second, how the presence of ILM affects exchange-rate variability following unanticipated monetary shocks.

International labour mobility is assumed here to result from the behaviour of a utility maximiser consumer-worker (C-W), who has two options as far as employment is concerned: to work in his native country or to work abroad. The two types of work are taken to be imperfect substitutes due to differences in work satisfaction arising from work time. Indeed, if domestic residents are utility maximisers and have the option to 'work home' or 'work abroad', the domestic labour supply is shown to be sensitive to changes in the domestic wage rate as well as to the foreign wage rate in domestic consumer-price units. This gives rise to an additional role for the nominal exchange rate: changes in the nominal exchange rate will affect workers' choices both indirectly, through their impact on the domestic real consumption wage via the consumer price index (CPI), and, directly, by making domestic nominal wages more/less attractive relative to foreign wages in domestic-currency units. Changes, therefore, in monetary policy will affect both the direction and the volume of international flows of labour.

The rest of the chapter is organised as follows. In section 2 we derive a labour supply function in the presence of international mobility of labour. Section 3 presents the macroeconomic model. Section 4 analyses the long-run response of the economy to an unanticipated expansionary monetary policy, while section 5 examines the short run effects and the dynamics of adjustment. Section 6 contains conclusions.

2 Deriving a Labour Supply Function in the case of International Mobility of Labour

We consider a utility maximiser consumer-worker who has two options as far as employment is concerned: to work in his native country or to work abroad. We assume that the two types of work are imperfect substitutes due to differences in work-satisfaction arising from work time.

The notion of work-satisfaction is based on the following considerations:[1] work time not only brings disutility to the consumer-worker (C-W), but it also brings some satisfaction to him/her. That is, work time can be taken to have two distinct roles: first, an indirect one, i.e. it reduces leisure time and therefore it brings disutility to the C-W (as the standard model of labour supply assumes). Second, a direct role, i.e. it brings some satisfaction to the C-W which textbook models of labour supply ignore. The direct role of work time in the C-W's utility has been established by both economic theory and empirical evidence. Hamermesh (1974), for example, points to Hume's view of man seeking after indolence, pleasure and action which implies that each and every type of work has an element of satisfaction attached to it. Hayes (1971) argues that work time is not only a source of income but it also satisfies certain needs of the C-W such as the need for activity, the need for creativity, the need for social interaction and the need for self-actualisation. Freeman's (1978) longitudinal survey shows that work-satisfaction is a major determinant of labour market mobility.[2] Akerlof, Rose and Yellen (1988) also have shown that job switching and job satisfaction are closely related.

In the case of labour mobility among countries, where the utility maximiser consumer-worker has two options, namely to work in his native country or to work abroad, one may indeed expect that the C-W will view the two jobs as imperfect substitutes which will give him a different level of satisfaction. This is not only because of non-pecuniary differences between the two states of work, such as a different language, but also because of changes in the exchange rate. Irrespective of what the exchange rate regime is, there can be no guarantee that there will be no unanticipated movements in the exchange rate and thus changes in the domestic-currency purchasing power of wages earned abroad.

In our analysis, we shall assume that each of the two types of work has an element of satisfaction attached to it. Indeed, we shall make the following assumptions:

1   the consumer-worker is free to work in his country, offering H_1 units of his working time, or in another country (called 'abroad') offering H_2 units of working time. He is allowed to choose any combination of work at home and work abroad as long as he satisfies the constraint:

$$H_1 + H_2 + L = T$$

where L and T denote leisure time and total time per period, respectively.

2   The consumer-worker realises a cost for moving between countries which is assumed to be fixed at M.

3 The foreign wage and the foreign price are converted into domestic-currency units by the prevailing exchange rate E (defined as units of domestic currency per unit of foreign currency). Therefore, if P (P*) is the price of the home (foreign) good in domestic (foreign-currency) units, W (W*) the nominal domestic (foreign) wage in domestic-currency (foreign-currency) units, X (X*) the consumption of the domestic (foreign) commodity, Y unearned (or property) income[3] and V net property income defined as $V = Y-M$, the consumer-worker faces the following budget constraint:

$$W H_1 + W_1{}^* H_2 + V = P X + P_1{}^* X^*$$

where $W_1{}^* \equiv W^* E$, $P_1{}^* \equiv P^* E$.

Consider the consumer-worker's maximisation problem, assuming a Cobb-Douglas utility function and a budget constraint which takes into account property income (wealth). Ignoring, for simplicity, minimal consumption of leisure-goods in the utility function,[4] the C-W's evaluation of, or 'satisfaction' from, the two types of work can be specified as:

$$S = (H_1)^\delta (H_2)^\epsilon$$

with $\delta + \epsilon = 1$.

Thus,

$$U = U (L,X,X^*,H_1,H_2) = X^\alpha X^{*\beta} L^\gamma S^\theta, \qquad \alpha+\beta+\gamma+\theta = 1$$

and the maximisation problem is

$$\max_{H_1, H_2} U = X^\alpha X^{*\beta} L^\gamma (H_1)^{\theta\delta} (H_2)^{\theta\epsilon}$$

subject to: $T = L + \Pi_1 + \Pi_2$

$$WH_1 + W_1{}^* H_2 + V = PX + P_1{}^* X^*$$

or, equivalently,

$$\text{max } U = X^\alpha \, X^{*\beta} \, (T\text{-}H_1\text{-}H_2)^\gamma \, (H_1)^{\theta\delta} \, (H_2)^{\theta\epsilon}$$
$$H_1,H_2$$

$$\text{s.t. } WH_1 + W_1^* H_2 + V = PX + P_1^* X^*.$$

The first-order conditions for a maximum are:

$$\frac{\alpha}{X} - \lambda P = 0$$

$$\frac{\beta}{X^*} - \lambda P_1^* = 0$$

$$\frac{\gamma}{L} - \frac{\theta\delta}{H_1} - \lambda W = 0$$

$$\frac{\gamma}{L} - \frac{\theta\epsilon}{H_2} - \lambda W_1^* = 0$$

As we show in the appendix, differentiating the first-order conditions we may sign the two labour-supply functions and the two goods-demand functions as follows

$$H_1 = \Psi \ \overset{+}{(} W, \overset{-}{W_1^*}, \overset{-}{P}, \overset{-}{P_1^*})$$

$$H_2 = \Phi \ (\overset{-}{W}, \overset{+}{W_1^*}, \overset{-}{P}, \overset{-}{P_1^*})$$

$$X = X \ (\overset{+}{W}, \overset{+}{W_1^*}, \overset{-}{P}, \overset{+}{P_1^*})$$

$$X^* = X^* \ (\overset{+}{W}, \overset{+}{W_1^*}, \overset{+}{P}, \overset{-}{P_1^*})$$

Also, as shown in the appendix, under the assumption that the worker's satisfaction from offering one unit of work at home is higher than the satisfaction he gets from offering one unit of work abroad, we can take the response of the domestic labour supply to the domestic wage to be larger than the response to the foreign wage, i.e. $|\Psi_1| > |\Psi_2|$.

3   The Macroeconomic Model

As shown in the previous section, the domestic labour supply derived from a Cobb-Douglas utility function can be taken to be an increasing function of the domestic nominal wage rate and a decreasing function of the foreign nominal wage, of the domestic price level and of the foreign price level. That is

$$H_1 = \Psi\,(W, W_1{}^*, P, P_1{}^*\,),\ \Psi_1 > 0,\ \Psi_2, \Psi_3, \Psi_4 < 0,\ |\Psi_1| > |\Psi_2| \qquad (1)$$

Since we focus on a small open economy, we can make the assumption that foreign residents are not allowed to work in the home economy, that is, total domestic labour supply equals the labour supply of domestic residents:

$$L^S \equiv \Psi\,(W, W_1{}^*, P, P_1{}^*) \qquad (2)$$

On the assumption of homothetic preferences (a Cobb-Douglas utility function), the share of each good in total expenditure is constant. So one may approximate the effect of changes in P and $P_1{}^*$ on $L^S \equiv \Psi\,(.)$ by incorporating into (2) a consumer- price index (CPI) of the form:

$$P_i = P^\lambda\,(EP^*)^{(1-\lambda)} \qquad (3)$$

where λ is the share of domestic goods in total domestic consumption,[5] which, as is conventional in the open economy macro literature, is taken to be greater than $\frac{1}{2}$.

Thus,

$$L^S \equiv \Psi\,(W, W^*, P_i)$$

and, on the assumption of no money illusion, we may write :

$$L^S \equiv \Psi\,(\frac{W}{P_i}, \frac{W_1{}^*}{P_i}),\ \Psi_1 > 0,\ \Psi_2 < 0,\ |\Psi_1| > |\Psi_2| \qquad (4)$$

Log-linearising the labour supply function (4) around steady-state equilibrium, we may write

$$\ell^S - c_1\,(w\text{-}p_i\,) - c_2\,(w_1{}^*\text{-}p_i),\ c_1, c_2 > 0,\ c_1 > c_2 \qquad (5)$$

Also, log-linearizing (3) and substituting into (5) we have

$$\ell^S = c_1\,(w\text{-}p) - c_3 s \qquad (6)$$

where

$$c_3 = \lambda c_2 + (1-\lambda)c_1 \text{ and } s = e + p^* - p \text{ is the real exchange rate.}$$

To derive a labour demand function we assume the following Cobb-Douglas production function

$$Q = L^a \qquad 0 < a < 1 \tag{7}$$

where the capital stock is taken to be fixed and, for notational simplicity, has been set equal to unity. Assuming that firms operate under conditions of perfect competition and that they pursue maximisation of profits, the labour demand function in logs is

$$\ell^d = -\epsilon(w-p) + \epsilon_1 \tag{8}$$

where

$$\epsilon = 1/(1-a) > 1, \qquad \epsilon_1 = \epsilon \ln a$$

At this point two features of (6) and (8) should be noted. First, firms are concerned with real product wages while workers are concerned about real consumption wages. Thus, while both (6) and (8) depend on the real product wage $(w-p)$, the labour supply function also depends on the real exchange rate. Suppose, for example, that the real exchange rate depreciates. This will increase the consumer price index. So workers will reduce their labour supply:[6] in terms of Figure 1.1, a real exchange rate depreciation will shift the labour supply curve to the left along an unshifted labour demand curve. Second, the presence of international labour mobility is identified with a non-zero value for the parameter c_2. A non-zero c_2 increases the responsiveness of labour supply to changes in the real exchange rate. This is because any given real exchange rate depreciation increases foreign nominal wages in domestic-currency units and thus induces home residents to switch work time from 'work home' to 'work abroad'.

Labour market equilibrium requires that $\ell^d = \ell^s = \ell$. Solving (6) and (8) for w and ℓ we obtain

$$w = p + \psi s + \frac{\epsilon_1}{\epsilon + c_1} \tag{9}$$

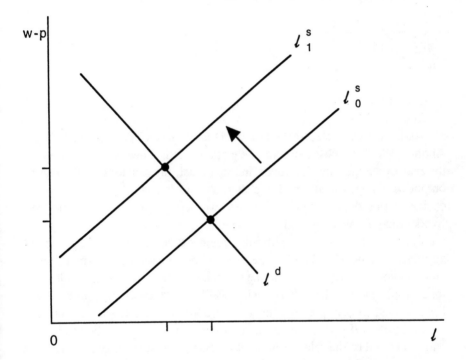

Figure 1.1   Home labour market and real exchange rate depreciation

$$\ell = - \psi \epsilon\, s + \frac{c_1\, \epsilon}{\epsilon + c_1} \tag{10}$$

where

$$\psi = c_3/(\epsilon + c_1)$$

Substituting (10) into the production function we have

$$q = -\alpha \psi s + \frac{a c_1\, \epsilon}{c_1 + \epsilon} \tag{11}$$

where

$$\alpha = a\, \epsilon > 0$$

As in, for example, Sachs (1980), Driskill and McCafferty (1987) and Ahtiala (1989), domestic output in equation (11) is a decreasing function of the real exchange rate. However, in our model, the sensitivity of domestic output to changes in the real exchange rate is stronger,[7] given that a real exchange rate depreciation will induce workers to switch work time from 'work home' to 'work abroad'.

In the goods market, equilibrium requires domestic production to equal aggregate demand, which is the sum of private domestic spending, I, government expenditure, G, and the net trade balance surplus, T.[8] Following, for example, Dornbush (1976a), Sachs (1980) and Devereux and Purvis (1990), I is assumed to be a positive function of domestic output and real private-sector wealth, Z/P_i. The trade balance surplus is a positive function of foreign output Q* and of the relative price of domestic and foreign goods, (EP*/P), and a negative function of domestic output:

$$Q = I(Q, Z/P_i) + G + T(Q, Q^*, EP^*/P) \tag{12}$$

$$T_1 < 0, \qquad I_1, I_2, T_2, T_3 > 0$$

Nominal private-sector wealth consists of three components: domestic money M, holdings of domestic bonds B and holdings of foreign bonds H:

$$Z = M + B + EH \tag{13}$$

Following, for example, Eaton and Turnovsky (1983), we take the following log-linear approximation to Z:

$$z = (1-\mu)\{um + (1-u)b\} + \mu(e+h) \tag{13a}$$

where μ is the share of foreign assets in total wealth and $(1-\mu)$ is the share of domestic assets in Z (in the neighbourhood of the steady state). We shall make the reasonable assumption that the share of domestic assets in total wealth is greater than that of the foreign assets, so that $0 < \mu < \frac{1}{2}$. We shall also assume a balanced budget. This implies that the stock of government bonds, b, remains invariant over time. Thus, in log-linear form, aggregate demand can be written as

$$q = \gamma_1(z-p_i) + \gamma_2 g + \gamma_3 t \tag{14}$$

where

$$t = -\theta_1 q + \theta_2 q^* + \theta_3 s$$

The demand for real money balances depends positively on a transaction variable, proxied by the volume of domestic output, and negatively on the opportunity cost of holding non-interest bearing assets in domestic currency, i.e. the rate of return on domestc bonds r:

$$m - p = \varphi q - br \tag{15}$$

Assuming perfect substitutability between domestic and foreign bonds, a standard interest-arbitrage condition is given by (16)

$$\dot{e}^e = r - r^* \tag{16}$$

The dynamics that drive this economy from one equilibrium to another and towards steady state is the accumulation or decumulation of foreign assets holdings through current account imbalances:

$$E\dot{H} = PT(.)$$

In log-linear form, the foreign-assets accumulation equation can be written as

$$\dot{h} = -\theta_1 q + \theta_3 s$$

or, equivalently using (11), as

$$\dot{h} = \sigma s \tag{17}$$

where

$$\sigma = \theta_1 \alpha \psi + \theta_3$$

To complete the model we introduce equation (18) which reflects the assumption of forward-looking expectations:

$$\dot{e}^e = \dot{e} \tag{18}$$

We shall focus on the effects on the domestic economy of an unanticipated domestic monetary expansion achieved via an open market operation. That is, we shall assume that the government buys domestic bonds from the private sector in exchange for money balances. This implies that the total stock of domestic assets held by the domestic private-sector remains unchanged.

4   Long-run Effects of an Unanticipated Monetary Expansion

Before considering the short-run response of the economy to the monetary expansion, it is useful to first examine the steady-state properties of the model. Steady-state equilibrium requires that $\dot{h} = \dot{e} = 0$. Imposing these conditions and totally differentiating (11)–(17) yields the following expressions for the long-run effects of the unanticipated monetary expansion.[9, 10]

$$\frac{d\bar{q}}{dm} = \frac{d\bar{s}}{dm} = 0 \tag{19}$$

$$\frac{d\bar{z}}{dm} = \frac{d\bar{p}}{dm} = \frac{d\bar{p_i}}{dm} = \frac{d\bar{w}}{dm} = 1 \tag{20}$$

$$\frac{d\bar{h}}{dm} = \frac{1 - \mu}{\mu} \quad (>1) \tag{21}$$

To understand these results note that in the new steady state, holdings of foreign assets must be neither rising nor falling. From (17), this implies that the real exchange rate has to remain unchanged in the new steady state. This in turn implies that domestic output has to remain unchanged.

Since in the new steady state the expected rate of exchange-rate depreciation must be zero, (16) implies that the domestic nominal interest rate must return to its initial steady state level. With an unchanged long-run r and an unchanged q, (15) requires the long-run domestic price level, p, to increase by the same amount as the increase in m to maintain equilibrium in the money market. Also, to keep an unchanged real exchange rate, the nominal exchange rate has to increase by the same amount as the domestic money supply. The increases in e and p result in a proportional increase in the long-run CPI, p_i.

With q and s remaining unchanged, goods market equilibrium requires an unchanged long-run real private-sector wealth. This implies that the private-sector's nominal wealth has to increase by the same amount as the consumer price index. Accordingly, domestic holdings of foreign bonds must increase in the new long run.

Finally, the long-run nominal wage rate increases by the same amount as the domestic price level and thus the real wage rate (both in consumption units and in production units) remains unchanged. Note that an unanticipated monetary expansion has no effect on the home country's steady-state output and real exchange rate with or without international labour mobility. Also, with or without international labour mobility, in the long run real wealth and real wage rates will return to their initial equilibrium levels. International labour mobility, however, may affect the short-run responses of domestic macroeconomic variables to the monetary expansion.

5   Short Run Effects and the Dynamics of Adjustment

To consider the role of international labour mobility in the behaviour of the economy between steady states it is convenient to express the variables of the model as deviations from their long-run equilibrium values. Ignoring, for simplicity, the effect of changes in the real exchange rate on aggregate demand through real wealth[11] we can write equations (11) and (14)–(18) in deviation forms as:

$$\hat{q} = -\alpha\psi\hat{s} \tag{22}$$

$$\eta\hat{q} + \gamma_1(1-\mu)\hat{p} = \nu\hat{s} + \xi\hat{h} \tag{23}$$

$$-\varphi\hat{q} - \hat{p} + b\hat{r} = 0 \tag{24}$$

$$\hat{e} = \hat{r} \tag{25}$$

$$\hat{h} = \sigma\hat{s} \tag{26}$$

where

$$\eta = 1 + \gamma_3\theta_1, \qquad \nu = \xi + \gamma_3\theta_3, \qquad \xi = \gamma_1\mu.$$

Substituting (22) into (23) and (24), we have

$$-\eta\alpha\psi\hat{s} + \gamma_1(1-\mu)\hat{p} = \nu\hat{s} + \xi\hat{h} \tag{27}$$

$$\alpha\varphi\psi\hat{s} - \hat{p} + b\hat{r} = 0 \tag{28}$$

Since $\hat{p} = \hat{e} - \hat{s}$, we may write (27)–(28) as

$$-[\eta\alpha\psi + \nu + \gamma_1(1-\mu)]\hat{s} = \xi\hat{h} - \gamma_1(1-\mu)\hat{e} \tag{29}$$

$$[1 + \alpha\varphi\psi]\hat{s} + b\hat{r} = \hat{e} \tag{30}$$

Solving (29)–(30) for $\hat{s}$ and $\hat{r}$ and inserting the resulting expressions into (25)–(26), we can write the model as a second-order differential equation system in e and h:

$$\begin{bmatrix} \hat{e} \\ \hat{h} \end{bmatrix} = \Delta^{-1} \begin{bmatrix} b_{11} & b_{12} \\ b_{21} & b_{22} \end{bmatrix} \begin{bmatrix} \hat{e} \\ \hat{h} \end{bmatrix} \tag{31}$$

where

$$b_{11} = \nu + \alpha\psi[\eta - \varphi\,\gamma_1(1-\mu)] \; (> 0)$$

$$b_{12} = \gamma_1\mu(1 + \alpha\varphi\psi) > 0$$

$$b_{21} = \sigma b\gamma_1(1-\mu) > 0$$

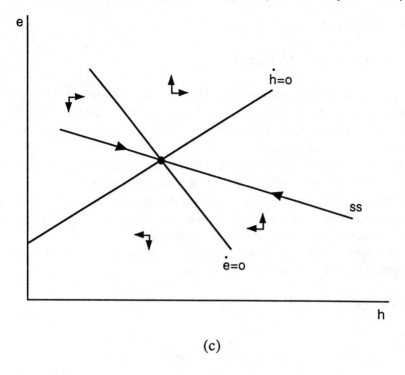

(c)

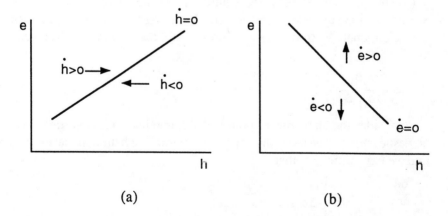

(a)   (b)

Figure 1.2   The nominal exchange rate and the stock of foreign bonds under rational expectations: deriving the saddle path

$b_{22} = -\sigma b \xi < 0$

$\Delta = b[\eta \alpha \psi + \nu + \gamma_1(1-\mu)] > 0$

Since h is a predetermined variable while e is a non-predetermined variable, unique convergence requires the equilibrium to be a saddle-point. This condition is satisfied here as the determinant of the state matrix of (31) is negative, i.e. $b_{11}b_{22}-b_{12}b_{21} < 0$.

To consider the effects of the monetary expansion on the dynamics of the nominal exchange rate under ILM, (31) has been plotted in Figure 1.2. The $\dot{h} = 0$ locus is upward sloping and its position and slope are unaffected by international mobility of labour. The $\dot{e} = 0$ locus can be taken to be downwards sloping, since the sign of b_{11} is almost certainly positive.

An algebraic expression for the unique stable path SS can be obtained by noting that the solution to (31) is of the form:

$$\hat{e} = V_1 e^{\rho_1 t} + V_2 e^{\rho_2 t} \tag{32}$$

$$\hat{h} = V_1 \left(\frac{\rho_1 - b_{11}}{b_{12}}\right) e^{\rho_1 t} + V_2 \left(\frac{\rho_2 - b_{11}}{b_{12}}\right) e^{\rho_2 t} \tag{33}$$

where $e^{\rho_i t} = \exp(\rho_i t)$. ρ_1 denotes the stable root, while ρ_2 is the unstable one, associated with the non-predetermined exchange rate. Restricting the solution to (31) to that on the stable path, requires the coefficient of the unstable root, V_2 in (32)–(33) to be set equal to zero. Imposing this condition, and using (33) to eliminate V_1 from (32), an expression for the SS locus can be obtained as

$$\hat{e} = -\frac{b_{12}}{(b_{11} - \Delta \rho_1)} \hat{h} \tag{34}$$

Consider the short-run response of the nominal exchange rate and of domestic output to the monetary expansion. Starting with the nominal exchange rate we have from (34) that

$$\frac{de}{dm} = 1 + \frac{b_{12}}{(b_{11} - \Delta \rho_1)} \left(\frac{1-\mu}{\mu}\right) > 1 \tag{35}$$

Since $\mu < 0.5$, $b_{12} > 0$ and $b_{11} - \rho_1 > 0$ the second term in (35) is positive, implying that an unanticipated monetary expansion will cause an initial

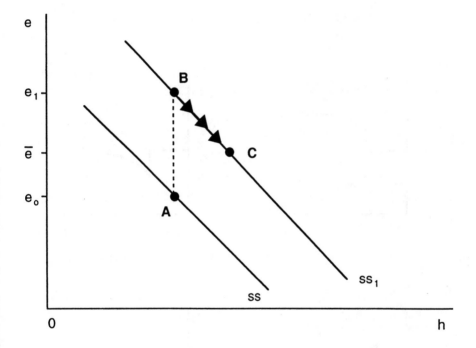

Figure 1.3   The nominal exchange rate and stock of foreign bonds responses (under rational expectations) to an unanticipated domestic monetary expansion

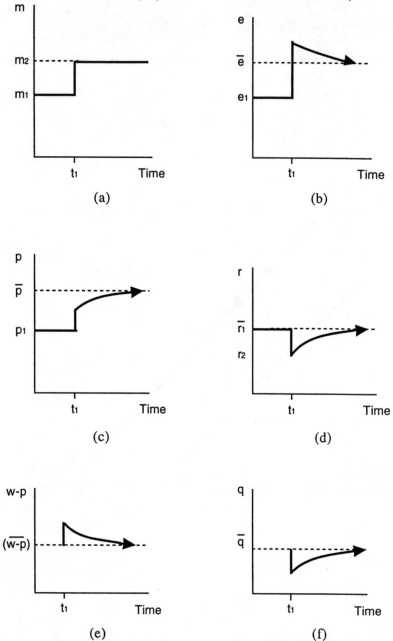

Figure 1.4   Paths of adjustment of money supply; nominal exchange rate; price level; interest rate; real product wage and output

nominal exchange rate depreciation which will exceed the long-run depreciation. This is illustrated in Figure 1.3. Initial equilibrium is at point A. Upon the unanticipated monetary expansion the SS locus shifts to SS_1: the nominal exchange rate depreciates in the short run to e_1 and adjusts slowly over time along the new stable locus SS_1 towards its new steady state value e.

To see why this is so, it is worth recalling the long-run effects of the monetary expansion. In the long run the stock of foreign bonds held by home residents will increase. Accordingly, accumulation of foreign bonds should take place over time. The accumulation of foreign bonds requires a trade-balance surplus. This is possible only through a short-run real exchange rate depreciation. But a short-run real exchange rate depreciation will affect equilibrium in the goods market: first, domestic output will fall; second, the domestic-currency value of foreign assets and thus private sector nominal wealth will increase. The first effect will increase the excess supply in the money market generated by the monetary expansion and both effects will serve to create an excess demand in the goods market. As a result, the price of home goods will have to rise. This rise in p, however, will not be large enough to restore short-run equilibrium in the money market: over time the stock of foreign bonds held by home residents, and hence their nominal wealth, will rise and this will require a rising domestic price level to maintain equilibrium. Since p has to increase during the adjustment period, its increase in the short run must be smaller than the increase in the money supply (see Figure 1.4c). Thus, in the short run, an excess supply will prevail in the money market requiring the domestic interest rate to fall in the short run relative to its long-run value to maintain equilibrium (see Figure 1.4d). Since r and $\dot{e}^e$ are constrained to move in the same direction through the bond-market equilibrium condition, the fall in r implies that expectations of future appreciation must be established. As the exchange rate has to depreciate in the new steady state, this can only occur through an initial depreciation that exceeds the long-run depreciation. Therefore, the nominal exchange rate overshoots its long-run equilibrium value and the real exchange rate depreciates. This leads to a fall in domestic output and a surplus in the trade balance.

Let us now consider the role of international labour mobility in the short-run response of output and the real exchange rate to the monetary-policy change. Substituting the reduced form equation (29) into (11) we obtain the following expression for the short run effect on q of the monetary expansion:

$$\hat{q}(0) = -\alpha\psi/\Delta \ \{\gamma_1 b(1-\mu)\hat{e}(0) - b\gamma_1\mu \ \hat{h}(0)\} \tag{36}$$

The presence of ILM affects the size of the short-run change in domestic output through two channels. First, directly, because it increases the responsiveness of q to any given change in e or h. This is reflected in the term $\alpha\psi/\Delta$. Second, indirectly, because it may affect the size of the short-run change in the nominal exchange rate. Since we know that an unanticipated monetary expansion leads in the short run to exchange-rate overshooting with or without ILM, we may assume that the direct effect is most likely to dominate, in which case the fall in domestic output will be larger with ILM: a nominal exchange rate depreciation not only will reduce the real domestic wage rate through its impact on consumer prices thus inducing workers to offer less work time, but it will also give incentives to workers to switch work time from 'work home' to 'work abroad'. This will result in a larger fall in domestic output.

Consider next the short-run response of the exchange rate. The presence of the second term in (35) is not determined by international labour mobility, implying that the presence of ILM is irrelevant for determining whether or not an unanticipated monetary expansion will create an excess supply in the money market. However, ILM may increase or decrease the size of the excess supply in the money market and therefore the size of the overshooting of the nominal exchange rate. Indeed, in the presence of ILM, any given real exchange rate depreciation will lead to a larger fall in output (output effect) and to larger increase in the trade balance surplus (trade balance effect). The output effect will increase the excess supply in the money market, created by the expansionary monetary policy. On the other hand, both effects will lead to a larger excess demand for domestic goods, thus resulting in a larger increase in the domestic-goods price (price effect). The price effect of ILM will, in turn, reduce the excess supply in the money market. Since the output effect and the price effect of international labour mobility operate in opposite directions, the overall impact of ILM on the size of the excess supply in the money market will depend on the relative magnitude of these two effects. If the increase in domestic- goods prices is greater than the fall in output, then ILM will reduce the size of the excess supply that will prevail in the money market. In this case, the nominal interest rate will have to fall in the short run by a relatively smaller amount. Therefore, in that case, the presence of international labour mobility will reduce the size of the required fall in $\dot{e}^e$, and so the extent to which the exchange rate must overshoot. This will be so when $\varphi\gamma_3\theta_3 + \varphi\gamma_1 - (1+\gamma_3\theta_1) < 0$. This case is illustrated in Figure 1.5a, where two stable loci are shown passing through an initial equilibrium point A: SS^{ILM} corresponding to the case of ILM and SS corresponding to that

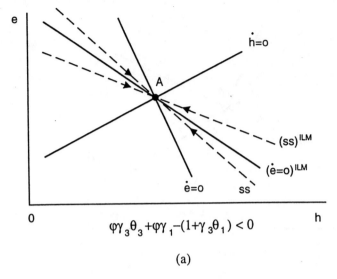

$$\varphi\gamma_3\theta_3 + \varphi\gamma_1 - (1+\gamma_3\theta_1) < 0$$

(a)

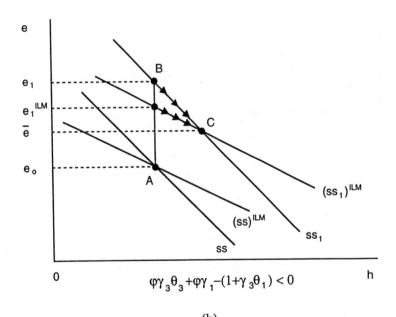

$$\varphi\gamma_3\theta_3 + \varphi\gamma_1 - (1+\gamma_3\theta_1) < 0$$

(b)

Figure 1.5 The nominal exchange rate and stock of foreign bonds responses to an unanticipated domestic monetary expansion with and without ILM: the less overshooting case

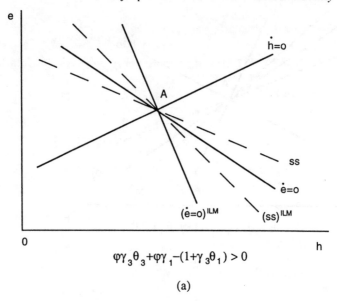

$$\varphi\gamma_3\theta_3+\varphi\gamma_1-(1+\gamma_3\theta_1)>0$$

(a)

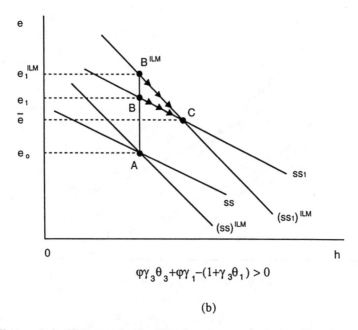

$$\varphi\gamma_3\theta_3+\varphi\gamma_1-(1+\gamma_3\theta_1)>0$$

(b)

Figure 1.6   The nominal exchange rate and stock of foreign bonds responses to an unanticipated domestic monetary expansion with and without ILM: the more overshooting case

without ILM: in the presence of international labour mobility the $e = 0$ locus will be less steep thus resulting in a flatter SS locus. Therefore, in Figure 1.5b, the unanticipated expansion in money supply will cause the nominal exchange rate to depreciate to e_1 in the absence of ILM and to e_1^{ILM} in the presence of ILM.

When, on the other hand, the unanticipated monetary expansion leads to a rise in p that is smaller than the fall in q, ILM will increase the size of the excess supply in the money market. In that case, the stable locus will be steeper with international mobility of labour, as illustrated in Figure 1.6a and b and the short-run nominal exchange rate depreciation will be larger in the presence of ILM than in the absence of ILM.

To illustrate the role of international labour mobility in the short-run response of the nominal exchange rate and of domestic output to the monetary expansion we solve the model numerically for a set of econometrically plausible parameter values.[12] Table 1.1 shows the impact effects on e and q of the unanticipated monetary expansion in three cases: no ILM, moderate ILM and high ILM.

Table 1.1   Impact effects of an unanticipated one per cent increase in the money supply

	$e(0)$	$q(0)$
No ILM $C_1=1$ $\quad$ $C_2=0$	1.35722	-0.05515
Moderate ILM $C_1=1$ $\quad$ $C_2=0.4$	1.34719	-0.07933
High ILM $C_1=1$ $\quad$ $C_2=0.9$	1.33612	-0.10334

As the table shows, the higher is the ILM, i.e. the higher is the value of the parameter c_2, the smaller is the size of the nominal exchange rate overshooting and the larger is the size of the fall in domestic output.

The response of the economy to the unanticipated monetary expansion is also illustrated in Figures 1.4(a)–1.4(f). The expansionary monetary policy on impact leads to a rise in e, a relative smaller rise in p and a fall in r. The increase in p and s increase the real product wage and thus domestic output falls.

Over time, the stock of foreign bonds will rise, thus creating excess demand in the output market. The excess demand in the output market will cause domestic-goods price to increase further. The adjustment path will therefore be characterised by falling real money balances, a rising nominal interest rate and an appreciating exchange rate. Indeed, this is why the domestic interest rate has to fall immediately after the monetary expansion: it must fall in the short run, so that it can rise during the adjustment period as the stock of foreign-bond holdings by domestic residents rises.

6   Conclusions

In this chapter we have incorporated the possibility of international labour mobility into a macro model of a small open economy with a flexible exchange rate and a competitive labour market and explored its role in the adjustment of this economy to unanticipated changes in monetary policy. Our analysis shows that an unanticipated monetary expansion, by causing a real exchange rate depreciation, will on impact cause a fall in the domestic labour supply both because it will decrease the home real consumption wage and because it will increase the foreign real wage in domestic-currency purchasing-power units. That is, domestic workers will reduce their total supply of labour and will also undertake more work abroad. This will cause a large fall in domestic employment, and thus a large short-run drop in domestic output. This has a straightforward policy implication: as national labour markets become more integrated, any attempt by the government of a single country to surprise the public with an unanticipated monetary expansion will have a larger negative short-run influence on the domestic economy. On the other hand, our analysis shows that, unlike capital mobility, labour mobility has no unambiguous effect on exchange-rate volatility: the short-run response of the nominal exchange rate to an unanticipated expansionary monetary policy may or may not be larger with ILM.

Notes

1 The definition of job satisfaction in industrial psychology is 'a positive emotional state resulting from the appraisal of one's job' (see Locke, quoted by Freeman, 1978).

2 The concept of labour mobility may be conceived in three different ways: as the capacity or ability of workers to move from one job to the another, or into and out of employment, or into and out of labour force; as their willingness or propensity to make such moves, given the opportunity; and as their actual movement. See Parnes (1954).

3 Note that in the case of a Cobb-Douglas utility function, exclusion of unearned income from the budget constraint yields a perfectly inelastic labour supply curve. See Barzel and Mcdonald (1973) for a detailed analysis.

4 The theory of labour supply usually assumes a Stone-Geary utility function which takes into account the minimal required consumption of goods and the minimal required time (see e.g. Abbott and Ashenfelter, 1976; Killingsworth, 1983). The utility function we consider here is a Cobb-Douglas function. Alternatively, one may consider an augmented Stone-Geary utility function:

$$U = B_0\ln(X-\gamma_1)+ B_1\ln(X^*-\gamma_2)+ B_2\ln(L-\gamma_3) + B_3\ln(H_1-\gamma_4) + B_3\ln(H_2-\gamma_5)$$

where $B_0+B_1+B_2+B_3+B_4 = 1$ and γ_i is the minimal required consumption of each 'good'. This utility function gives results which are very similar to those obtained in the main text. However, here, there are five parameters, i.e. γ_1, γ_2, γ_3, γ_4 and γ_5, that affect the labour supplies.

5 $\lambda = \alpha/(\alpha+\beta)$ for the Cobb-Douglas utility we consider in section 2.

6 $\ell^S = c_1 w - c_2(w^*+e) - (c_1-c_2) [p+(1-\lambda)s]$, and $c_1 > c_2$.

7 Note that, from equation (11), we have

$$\frac{d\psi}{dc_2} = \frac{\lambda}{c_1 + \epsilon} > 0.$$

8 Following, e.g. Driskill and McCafferty (1987) we assume that net payments on foreign debt are small enough to be ignored and thus that the current account can be taken to be equal to the net trade surplus.

9 Note that the long run effects of the monetary expansion and thus the expressions in (19)–(21), are derived on the assumption that $dm = - (1-u)/u\, db$.

10 Note that

$$\frac{d\bar{h}}{dm} = \frac{1-\mu}{\mu} > 1.$$

This relationship says that any monetary expansion will drive the economy towards a new steady-state point below the 45° line in the (e,h) space.

11 As long as $\gamma_3\theta_3 + \gamma_1\mu - \gamma_1 (1-\lambda) > 0$, this assumption does not change our qualitative results.

12 To solve the model numerically, we have assumed the following non-ILM parameter values which are similar to much of the existing macro-literature, including Bhandari and Genberg (1989), Zervoyianni (1992) and Van der Ploeg (1995):

$$a = \gamma_1 = \gamma_3 = \theta_1 = \theta_3 = \tfrac{1}{2}, \mu = 0.4, b = 2, \varphi = 1, \lambda = 0.7.$$

Appendix

The first order conditions are:

$$\frac{\gamma}{L} - \frac{\theta\delta}{H_1} - \lambda W = 0$$

$$\frac{\gamma}{L} - \frac{\theta\epsilon}{H_2} - \lambda W_1^* = 0$$

$$\frac{\alpha}{X} - \lambda P = 0$$

$$\frac{\beta}{X^*} - \lambda P_1^* = 0$$

$$W H_1 + W_1^* H_2 + V = P X + P_1^* X^*$$

Differentiating the first-order conditions and the budget constraint, we obtain

$$
\begin{bmatrix}
\xi_1 & K & 0 & 0 & W \\
K & \xi_2 & 0 & 0 & W_1^* \\
0 & 0 & -\alpha/X^2 & 0 & -P \\
0 & 0 & 0 & -\beta/X^{*2} & -P_1^* \\
W & W_1^* & -P & -P_1^* & 0
\end{bmatrix}
\begin{bmatrix}
dH_1 \\
dH_2 \\
dX \\
dX^* \\
d\lambda
\end{bmatrix}
=
\begin{bmatrix}
-\lambda dW \\
-\lambda dW_1^* \\
\lambda dP \\
\lambda dP_1^* \\
dj
\end{bmatrix}
$$

where

$$dJ = -dV - H_1 dW - H_2 dW_1^* + X dP + X^* dP_1^*$$

$$\xi_1 = K - (\theta\delta)/H_1^2 < 0$$

$$\xi_2 = K - (\theta\epsilon)/H_2^2 < 0$$

$$K = -(\gamma/L^2) < 0$$

Solving the above system for the substitution effect by setting dJ=0, we obtain

$$
\begin{bmatrix} dH_1 \\ dH_2 \\ dX \\ dX^* \end{bmatrix} = (\det)^{-1}
\begin{bmatrix}
a_1 & a_2 & a_3 & a_4 \\
a_2 & b_2 & b_3 & b_4 \\
-a_3 & -b_3 & c_3 & c_4 \\
-a_4 & -b_4 & c_4 & d_4
\end{bmatrix}
\begin{bmatrix} dW \\ dW_1{}^* \\ dP \\ dP_1{}^* \end{bmatrix}
$$

where

$$(\det) = -\left\{ \frac{\alpha\beta\Phi}{X^2 X^{*2}} - 1/\lambda(PX+P_1{}^* X^*)(\xi_1\xi_2 - K^2) \right\} > 0$$

$$a_1 = -\frac{\alpha\beta}{X^2 X^{*2}} \left\{ (PX+P_1{}^* X^*)\xi_2 - \lambda W_1{}^{*2} \right\} > 0$$

$$a_2 = \frac{\alpha\beta}{X^2 X^{*2}} \left\{ (PX+P_1{}^* X^*)K - \lambda WW_1{}^* \right\} < 0$$

$$a_3 = \frac{\beta\lambda P}{X^{*2}} \left\{ W\xi_2 - W_1{}^* K \right\} \gtreqless 0$$

$$a_4 = \frac{\alpha\lambda P_1{}^*}{X^2} \left\{ W\xi_2 - W_1{}^* K \right\} \gtreqless 0$$

$$b_2 = -\frac{\alpha\beta}{X^2 X^{*2}} \left\{ (PX+P_1{}^* X^*)\xi_1 - \lambda W^2 \right\} > 0$$

$$b_3 = \frac{\beta\lambda P}{X^{*2}} \left\{ W_1{}^* \xi_1 - KW \right\} \gtreqless 0$$

$$b_4 = \frac{\alpha\lambda P_1{}^*}{X^2} \left\{ W_1{}^* \xi_1 - KW \right\} \gtreqless 0$$

$$c_3 = \frac{\beta\lambda\Phi}{X^{*2}} - \lambda(P_1{}^*)^2 (\xi_1\xi_2 - K^2) \right\} < 0$$

$$c_4 = PP_1^* (\xi_1\xi_2 - K^2) > 0$$

$$d_4 = \frac{\alpha\lambda\Phi}{X^2} - \lambda P^2(\xi_1\xi_2 - K^2) < 0$$

$$\Phi = W^2\xi_2 - 2WW_1^* K + (W_1^*)^2 \xi_1 < 0$$

$$\xi_1 = K - (\theta\delta)/H_1^2 < 0$$

$$\xi_2 = K - (\theta\epsilon)/H_2^2 < 0$$

$$K = - (\gamma/L^2) < 0$$

The expressions c_3 and d_4 are negative since

$$\Phi = W^2\xi_2 - 2WW_1^*K + (W_1^*)^2 \xi_1 = K(W- W_1^*)^2 - \{(\epsilon\theta W^2)/H_2^2 + $$
$$+ (\delta\theta W_1^{*2})/H_1^2\} < 0$$

and $\xi_1\xi_2 - K^2 > 0$,

given that $\xi_1 < 0$, $\xi_2 < 0$, $K < 0$ and K is included in ξ_1 and ξ_2.

The signs of the expressions a_3, a_4, b_3 and b_4 are in general ambiguous. However, assuming that at the initial steady state the two wages are equal in terms of purchasing power, we may sign these expressions as negative, since

$$\{W\xi_2 - W_1^* K\} = -(\gamma/L^2) (W-W_1^*) - W\theta\epsilon/(H_2^2)$$

$$\{W_1^* \xi_1 - KW\} = (\gamma/L^2) (W-W_1^*) - W_1^* \theta\delta/(H_1^2)$$

Finally, assuming that that the worker's satisfaction from offering one unit of work at home is higher to the satisfaction he gets from offering one unit of work abroad, i.e $\delta/H_1 > \epsilon/H_2$, we can expect that the response of the domestic labour supply to the domestic wage exceeds the response to the foreign wage. That is $|\Psi_1| > |\Psi_2|$

since

$$\frac{dH_1}{dW} + \frac{dH_1}{dW_1^*} = \frac{\alpha\beta}{(\det)X^2X^{*2}} \{\theta\epsilon/H_2^2(PX+P_1^* X^*)+W_1^*\theta[\delta/H_1-\epsilon/H_2]\} > 0$$

The two supply functions and the two demand functions are:

$$H_1 = \Psi\ (\overset{+}{W},\ \overset{-}{W}_1{}^*,\ \overset{-}{P},\ \overset{-}{P}_1{}^*)$$

$$H_2 = \Phi\ (\overset{-}{W},\ \overset{+}{W}_1{}^*,\ \overset{-}{P},\ \overset{-}{P}_1{}^*)$$

$$X = X\ (\overset{+}{W},\ \overset{+}{W}_1{}^*,\ \overset{-}{P},\ \overset{+}{P}_1{}^*)$$

$$X^* = X^*(\overset{+}{W},\ \overset{+}{W}_1{}^*,\ \overset{+}{P},\ \overset{-}{P}_1{}^*)$$

2 Transmission of Fiscal Disturbances Between Countries and International Migration

1   Introduction

In chapter 1 we considered a small open economy which operated under conditions of international labour mobility. In that model labour mobility was generated by changes in the real exchange rate, and we assumed that inflows and outflows of labour could be realised instantly. Thus, an unanticipated expansion in the domestic money supply, by causing a real exchange rate depreciation, immediately caused an outflow of labour which was reversed over time as the real exchange rate had to remain unchanged in the long run.

The purpose of this chapter is to explore the role of international migration of labour in the transmission of fiscal disturbances between countries. Indeed, here we extend our analysis in the previous chapter in three directions. First, we consider a world of two interdependent, symmetric, economies. Second, we assume that both economies operate under conditions of international migration of labour (IML) which we distinguish from international labour mobility (ILM) in that the former is a continuous process through time while the latter involves instantaneous adjustment. Third, we consider a fiscal contraction originated abroad and we investigate the role of IML in the transmission of this disturbance to the home country.

Much of the research on the transmission effects of fiscal disturbances across countries is carried out under the assumption of no international migration: see, for example, Allen and Kennen (1980), Mundell (1983), Argy and Salop (1983), Oudiz and Sachs (1984), McKibbin and Sachs (1986), Jensen (1991) and Van der Ploeg (1988, 1995). This literature assumes either that labour supply is a negative function of the real exchange rate, i.e. workers are concerned with the real purchasing power of their wages, or that labour supply is independent of the real exchange rate and nominal wage rigidity prevails in the labour market. In those models where labour supply is a negative function of the real exchange rate, each country's employment and output supply are also negative functions of the real exchange rate. This implies that fiscal-policy changes originated in one country are transmitted to the other countries' employment and output, through the real exchange rate. A fiscal expansion at home, for example, by appreciating the real exchange rate, will lead to higher home employment and output at the expense of lower foreign employment and output. Thus, fiscal expansion in one country is a beggar-thy-neighbour policy. In the case that labour supply is assumed to be independent of the real exchange rate and nominal wage rigidity prevails in the labour markets, as in a Mundell-Flemming world, the supply of output is a positive function of the prices of domestic goods. In this case, a fiscal expansion in one country will raise the price level in both countries[1] and thus, by reducing the real product wage, will raise output supply in each one of them.

To incorporate international migration into a two-country framework we follow the literature on labour migration in making three assumptions: first, that international migration is generated by real consumption-wage differentials between the two countries; second, that migration is a continuous process taking place over time; and, third, at any point in time, labour supply in each country is fixed by the past decisions of workers about migration and each country's workforce is fully employed. This last assumption, made often in the literature of international migration (see, for example, Burda and Wyplosz (1991) and Baldwin and Venables (1994)) is also made here for the purpose of analytical tractability.

With a fixed labour supply at any point in time and without nominal rigidities, an unanticipated foreign fiscal contraction will lead to a real exchange rate appreciation but will have no impact on employment and output at home and abroad, in the short run. Over time, however, the appreciation of the real exchange rate, by lowering the foreign real consumption wage relative to the home real consumption wage, will generate a net flow of labour from the foreign economy towards the home economy. As a result, each country's labour force will change: the home economy will experience an increase in its workforce at the expense of the foreign economy. Under conditions of full employment, this will lead to an increase in home output and a drop in foreign output. Thus, fiscal disturbances originated in one country will be transmitted over time to other countries through international labour migration. Moreover, real exchange-rate variability will be larger in the absence of IML than in the presence of IML.

The rest of the chapter is organised as follows. Section 2 focuses on the labour markets stating our assumptions about international migration. In section 3 we present the macroeconomic model. In section 4 we examine the steady-state properties of the model, while in section 5 we analyse its dynamics. In section 6 we analyse the impact and dynamic effects of an unanticipated foreign fiscal contraction, and in section 7 we investigate the role of IML in the results. Section 8 contains concluding comments.

2   Labour Markets and International Migration

Along the lines suggested by the labour migration literature, for example, Mortensen (1970), Harris-Todaro (1970), Lucas (1976), Bhagwati and Rodriguez (1975), Rodriguez (1976) and Nickell (1986), we shall make the following assumptions about the labour markets at home and abroad:

1   workers have two alternative 'work regimes': either to work in their own country or to work abroad;

2   from the view point of the workers these two alternative 'work regimes' differ only to the extent that they offer different real consumption wages. Thus, workers take the decision to leave or join one country's workforce on comparison of the two real consumption wages. This implies that the real consumption wage differential is the driving force of migration: a higher home real consumption wage relative to foreign real consumption wage will generate a flow of labour into the home country. By the symmetry assumption the other country will experience an outflow of labour;[2]

3   migration is a continuous process which takes place over time. This may be justified on the grounds that information about jobs is imperfect and must be obtained sequentially via a search process that takes time and that workers respond to this information within a time interval rather than instantaneously.[3] Accordingly, we may specify labour-supply-flow functions as differential equations, postulating a dynamic adjustment of each country's labour force driven by the existing real consumption wage differential;

4   at any point in time the demand for labour by a representative firm is determined by standard profit-maximisation conditions;

5   there are no nominal rigidities and wages and prices are fully flexible.

Given these assumptions and also utilizing the assumption that the two economies are symmetric, we may specify the equations which characterise the behaviour of labour markets as follows:

$$W_t^P = f(L_t) \qquad\qquad f_1 < 0 \qquad\qquad (1.\alpha_1)$$

$$\frac{dL}{dt}\,\frac{1}{L_t} = Z(W_t^c, W_t^{*c}),\, Z_1 > 0,\, Z_2 = -Z_1,\, < 0 \qquad (1.\alpha_2)$$

$$Z(W_t^c, W_t^{*c}) = 0,\, \text{for } \overline{W}_t^c = \overline{W}_t^{*c} \qquad\qquad (1.\alpha_3)$$

$$W_t^{*P} = f(L_t^*) \qquad\qquad\qquad\qquad\qquad (2.\alpha_1)$$

$$\frac{dL^*}{dt}\,\frac{1}{L_t^*} = -Z(W_t^c, W_t^{*c}) \qquad\qquad (2.\alpha_2)$$

where

$$W_t^P \equiv \left(\frac{W}{P}\right)_t \qquad \text{is the home real product wage}$$

$$W_t^{*P} \equiv \left(\frac{W^*}{P^*}\right)_t \qquad \text{is the foreign real product wage}$$

$$W_t^c \equiv W_t^P\, S^{-(1-\lambda)} \qquad \text{is the home real consumption wage}$$

$$W_t^{*c} \equiv W_t^{*P}\, S^{(1-\lambda)} \qquad \text{is the foreign real consumption wage}$$

S   is the real exchange rate (defined as the price of foreign goods in terms of home goods)

λ   is the share of home (foreign) goods in home (foreign) residents' aggregate expenditure. As is conventional in the open-economy macro literature, we assume the that home (foreign) residents have a preference for home (foreign) goods so that $\lambda > \frac{1}{2}$.

Equations ($1.\alpha_1$) and ($2.a_1$) are derived from profit-maximisation behaviour by firms: they state that at any point in time, real product wages and employment will be negatively related. Equations $(1.\alpha_2)$ and $(2.\alpha_2)$ are the flow supply of labour for the home country and the foreign country respectively. They state that an increase in the home real consumption wage relative to the foreign real consumption wage will generate over time labour flows from the foreign country to the home country. At any point in time labour supply in each country is fixed by the past decisions of workers about migration, and the two product wages are determined by the profit-maximisation conditions $(1.\alpha_1)$ and $(2.\alpha_1)$. Equation $(1.\alpha_3)$ states that no migration flows will take place when the two real consumption wages are equalised. Thus $(1.\alpha_3)$ is one of the conditions for long-run equilibrium in the two economies. To illustrate the above we make use of Figures 2.1 and 2.2.

Let us assume that initially, at time zero, both labour markets are in long-run equilibrium with employment levels L_0 and L_0^*. At employment levels L_0 and L_0^*, $(1.a_1)$ and $(2.a_1)$ determine the two product wages W_0^P and W_0^{*P}. Furthermore, let us assume that at time zero, the home real consumption wage increases. Since at time zero L_0 and thus W_0^P are fixed, increases in the home real consumption wage can occur only through a fall in the real exchange rate. This fall in the real exchange rate will lower the foreign real consumption wage and hence will create a real consumption wage differential in favour of the home economy. As a result, over time an outflow of labour from foreign economy towards home economy will take place. Thus changes in the real exchange rate, by creating migration flows, will change the long-run levels of employment and the real product wages of two countries. This has important macroeconomic implications: as we shall show shortly unilateral fiscal policy changes, by affecting the real exchange rate, will generate migration flows over time and will therefore change the employment levels and the production of output in both economies.

3   A Two-Country Macroeconomic Model with International Migration

In this section we incorporate log-linear versions of $(1.\alpha_1)$, $(1.\alpha_2)$, $(2.\alpha_1)$ and $(2.\alpha_2)$ into an explicit two-country macroeconomic model. Each country is assumed to produce a single good and to issue a single financial asset, to be called bond. Each country's good is taken to be an imperfect consumption substitute for the other country's good. Bonds are traded between the two

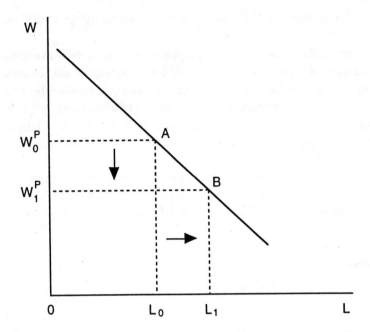

Figure 2.1 Home labour market and international migration

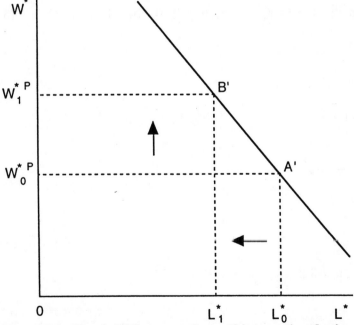

Figure 2.2 Foreign labour market and international migration

countries under conditions of perfect capital mobility and perfect substitutability.

As mentioned earlier, while at any point in time each country is assumed to have a fixed workforce, over time each country's labour supply may change due to migration flows induced by real wage differentials. Obviously, in a world of two symmetric economies and in the absence of labour force growth, an outflow of labour from one country matches exactly the inflow of labour to the other country. As a result, the world 'labour supply' in the model is fixed.

Equations (1)–(6) and (7)–(11) below describe the home economy and the foreign economy respectively. All variables, except for interest rates, are in logarithms and are specified as deviations from an initial steady-state equilibrium.

The home economy:

$$y = \varphi \ell \tag{1}$$

$$\omega^P = -(1-\varphi)\ell \tag{2}$$

$$y = b_1 S - b_2 r^R + b_3 y^* + g, \qquad b_1, b_2 > 0, \ 0 < b_3 < 1 \tag{3}$$

$$\dot{S} = r^R - r^{*R} \tag{4}$$

$$\dot{\ell} = -z\,(\omega^{*c} - \omega^c)\,, z > 0 \tag{5}$$

$$\omega^c = \omega^P - (1-\lambda)S, \qquad \tfrac{1}{2} < \lambda < 1 \tag{6}$$

The foreign economy:

$$y^* = \varphi \ell^* \tag{7}$$

$$\omega^{*P} = -(1-\varphi)\ell^* \tag{8}$$

$$y^* = -b_1 S - b_2 r^{*R} + b_3 y + g^* \tag{9}$$

$$\dot{\ell}^* = -\dot{\ell} \tag{10}$$

$$\omega^{*c} = \omega^{*p} + (1-\lambda)S \tag{11}$$

where

$\omega^p \equiv \omega - p$ and $\omega^{*p} \equiv \omega^* - p^*$.

Equations (1) and (7) describe the supply of output at home and abroad respectively, and are derived from log-linearisation of Cobb-Douglas production functions. Equations (2) and (8) are log-linear versions of $(1.\alpha_1)$ and $(2.\alpha_1)$. Equation (3) and (9) are IS curves: the aggregate demand for each country's output increases when the real interest rate or the relative price of domestic goods falls, when there is a domestic fiscal expansion, and when there is an expansion of output abroad. Equation (4) is the interest-rate parity condition when investors are engaged in risk-neutral arbitrage. Equations (5) and (10) describe the change over time in labour supply at home and abroad. Equations (6) and (11) are the definitions of the real consumption wage at home and abroad respectively.

Equations (1)–(11) constitute a third-order dynamic system in ℓ, ℓ^* and the real exchange rate S. While labour supply at home and abroad, ℓ and ℓ^*, adjust continuously everywhere, the real exchange rate is free to jump in response to unanticipated events.

Following Aoki (1981) we shall conduct the analysis of the dynamics by decomposing the model into sums and differences of the relevant variables. Accordingly, for any variable X we define X^w and X^d as

$$X^w = X + X^* \text{ and } X^d = X - X^*$$

The sums of the Xs represent 'global variables' while the differences of the Xs represent 'relative variables'. Thus the model described by equations (1)–(11) can be decomposed into two subsystems:

Sums:

$$y^w = \varphi\ell^w \tag{12}$$

$$\omega^{pw} = - (1-\varphi)\ell^w \tag{13}$$

$$\ell^w = 0 \tag{14}$$

$$y^w = - \gamma_1 r^w + \gamma_2 g^w, \tag{15}$$

$$\gamma_1 = b_2/(1-b_3) > 0, \quad \gamma_2 = 1/(1-b_3) > 0$$

$$\omega^{cw} = \omega^{pw} \tag{16}$$

Differences:

$$y^d = \varphi \ell^d \tag{17}$$

$$\omega^{pd} = - (1-\varphi)\ell^d \tag{18}$$

$$y^d = \delta_1 S - \delta_2 r^d + \delta_3 g^d, \tag{19}$$

$$\delta_1 = 2b_1/(1+b_3) > 0, \quad \delta_2 = b_2/(1+b_3) > 0 \quad \delta_3 = 1/(1+b_3) > 0$$

$$\dot{S} = r^d \tag{20}$$

$$\dot{\ell}^d = 2z\omega^{cd} \tag{21}$$

$$\omega^{cd} = \omega^{pd} - 2(1-\lambda)S \tag{22}$$

4   The Steady-state Properties of the Model

Since the dynamics of the model depend in part on the steady state, it is convenient to start by considering its steady-state properties. The steady-state is attained when $\dot{\ell} = \dot{\ell}* = \dot{S} = 0$ and therefore when there is no real-consumption -wage differentials. Imposing these conditions we obtain the equations:

$$\bar{r}^R = \bar{r}^{*R} \tag{23}$$

$$\bar{\omega}^c = \bar{\omega}^{*c} \tag{24}$$

$$\bar{y} = \varphi \bar{\ell} \tag{25}$$

$$\bar{y}* = \varphi \bar{\ell}* \tag{26}$$

$$\bar{\omega}^p = - (1-\varphi)\bar{\ell} \tag{27}$$

$$\overline{\omega}^{*p} = -(1-\varphi)\overline{\ell}* \tag{28}$$

$$\overline{y} = b_1\overline{S} - b_2\overline{r}^R + b_3\overline{y}^* + g, \tag{29}$$

$$\overline{y}^* = -b_1\overline{S} - b_2\overline{r}^{*R} + b_3\overline{y} + g^* \tag{30}$$

$$\overline{\omega}^c = \overline{\omega}^p - (1-\lambda)\overline{S} \tag{31}$$

$$\overline{\omega}^{*c} = \overline{\omega}^{*p} + (1-\lambda)\overline{S} \tag{32}$$

$$\overline{\ell} + \overline{\ell}* = 0 \tag{33}$$

Equations (23)–(33) form an 11-equation system in 11 unknowns: i.e. $\overline{y}$, $\overline{y}^*$, $\overline{\ell}, \overline{\ell}^*$, $\overline{r}^R$, $\overline{r}^{*R}$, $\overline{S}$, $\overline{\omega}^p$, $\overline{\omega}^{*p}$, $\overline{\omega}^c$, and $\overline{\omega}^{*c}$.[4] The solution to this system is:

$$\overline{S} = -\mu_1 (g-g^*) \tag{34}$$

$$\overline{\omega}^c = \overline{\omega}^{*c} = 0 \tag{35}$$

$$\overline{\ell} = \mu_3 (g-g^*) \tag{36}$$

$$\overline{\ell}* = -\mu_3 (g-g^*) \tag{37}$$

$$\overline{y} = \varphi\mu_3 (g-g^*) \tag{38}$$

$$\overline{y}^* = -\varphi\mu_3 (g-g^*) \tag{39}$$

$$\overline{\omega}^p = -\mu_4 (g-g^*) \tag{40}$$

$$\overline{\omega}^{*p} = \mu_4 (g-g^*) \tag{41}$$

$$\overline{r}^R = \overline{r}^{*R} = \mu_2 (g+g^*) \tag{42}$$

where

$$\mu_1 = (1-\varphi)/2\theta_4 > 0, \qquad \mu_2 = 1/2b_2 > 0, \qquad \mu_3 = (1-\lambda)/2\theta_4 > 0,$$

$$\mu_4 = (1-\lambda)(1-\varphi)/2\theta_4 > 0, \qquad \theta_4 = (1-\lambda)(1+b_3) + b_1(1-\varphi) > 0$$

A foreign fiscal contraction will reduce the home and foreign real interest rate by the same amount in the long run. Real consumption wages remain unchanged in the long run. This is due to two reasons. First, no real consumption wage differentials should exist in the steady state equilibrium, i.e. $\bar{\omega}^{cd} = \bar{\omega}^{c} - \bar{\omega}^{*c} = 0$. Second, since the world labour supply remains unchanged, the world real product wage also remains unchanged. But the latter is identical to the world real consumption wage in this model. With both $\bar{\omega}^{cd}$ and $\bar{\omega}^{cw}$ remaining unchanged, $\bar{\omega}^{c}$ and $\bar{\omega}^{*c}$ also remain unchanged in the long run.

The decrease in foreign government expenditure will cause a long-run real exchange rate appreciation. Since the long-run foreign (and the home) real consumption wage remains unaltered, the appreciation will be accompanied by a proportional rise in the long-run foreign real product wage ω^{*p}. From the firms' profit maximisation condition this implies that foreign employment must fall in the long run. Since world employment is fixed, the fall in $\bar{\ell}^{*}$ will be accompanied by an increase in $\bar{\ell}$. Hence, the unilateral fiscal contraction abroad will reduce foreign output and increase domestic output in the long run.

5   The Dynamics of the System

Because of the symmetry assumption, which implies that flows of labour into one country occur at the expense of the other country, the world economy is always in stationary equilibrium given by

$$y^{w} = \ell^{w} = \omega^{cw} = \omega^{pw} = 0 \tag{43}$$

As far as relative variables are concerned, through appropriate substitutions, the subsystem (17)–(22) can be expressed in terms of the dynamics of employment differentials and the real exchange rate:

$$\begin{bmatrix} \dot{S} \\ \dot{\ell}^{d} \end{bmatrix} = \begin{bmatrix} \theta_2 & -\theta_1 \\ -4z(1-\lambda) & -2z(1-\varphi) \end{bmatrix} \begin{bmatrix} S - \bar{S} \\ \ell^{d} - \bar{\ell}^{d} \end{bmatrix} \tag{44}$$

where

$$\theta_1 = \varphi(1+b_3)/b_2 > 0, \qquad \theta_2 = 2b_1/b_2 > 0$$

The determinant of the state matrix of (44), which equals

$$- 2z [(1-\varphi)\theta_2 + 2\theta_1 (1-\lambda)]$$

is negative implying that the equilibrium is a saddle point. Let ρ_1 denote the stable (negative) root and ρ_2 the unstable (positive) root. We assume that prior to the unanticipated foreign fiscal contraction both economies are in steady-state equilibrium with $\ell^* = \bar{\ell}_1{}^*$, $\ell = \bar{\ell}_1$ and $S = \bar{S}_1$. The new steady state corresponding to the disturbed system is

$$\ell^* = \bar{\ell}^*{}_2 = \bar{\ell}^*{}_1 + d\bar{\ell}^*, \ \ell= \bar{\ell}_2 = \bar{\ell}_1 + d\,\bar{\ell} \text{ and } S = \bar{S}_2 = \bar{S}_1 + d\bar{S}.$$

We focus our analysis on the bounded solution to (44) which we report in equations (45) and (46) below, while in the Appendix following Turnovsky (1986), we describe the steps involved in deriving it:

$$\ell^d = \bar{\ell}^d{}_2 - \frac{(1-\lambda)}{\theta_4}\ e^{\rho_1 t} \tag{45}$$

$$S = \bar{S}_2 + \frac{\theta_1 (1-\lambda)}{(\rho_1 - \theta_2)\theta_4}\ e^{\rho_1 t} \tag{46}$$

Since, for any variable X,

$$\hat{\bar{X}} = \tfrac{1}{2}\hat{X}^d \text{ and } \hat{\bar{X}}^* = -\tfrac{1}{2}\hat{X}^d$$

we have:

$$\ell = \bar{\ell}_2 - \frac{(1-\lambda)}{2\theta_4}\ e^{\rho_1 t} \tag{47}$$

$$\ell^* = \bar{\ell}^*{}_2 + \frac{(1-\lambda)}{2\theta_4}\ e^{\rho_1 t} \tag{48}$$

It follows from (1)–(11) that the paths of the other endogenous variables are given by

$$y = \bar{y}_2 - \frac{(1-\lambda)\varphi}{2\theta_4}\ e^{\rho_1 t} \tag{48.a}$$

$$y^* = \bar{y}^*_2 + \frac{(1-\lambda)\varphi}{2\theta_4}\, eP_1 t \tag{48.b}$$

$$\omega P = \bar{\omega}P_2 + \frac{(1-\lambda)\,(1-\varphi)}{2\theta_4}\, eP_1 t \tag{48.c}$$

$$\omega^* P = \bar{\omega}^* P_2 - \frac{(1-\lambda)\,(1-\varphi)}{2\theta_4}\, eP_1 t \tag{48.d}$$

$$\omega^c = \frac{(1-\lambda)\,[(1-\varphi)\,(P_1 - \theta_2) - 2\theta_1(1-\lambda)]}{2\theta_4\,(P_1 - \theta_2)}\, eP_1 t \tag{48.e}$$

$$\omega^{*c} = -\frac{(1-\lambda)\,[(1-\varphi)\,(P_1 - \theta_2) - 2\theta_1(1-\lambda)]}{2\theta_4\,(P_1 - \theta_2)}\, eP_1 t \tag{48.f}$$

$$r = \bar{r}_2 + \frac{\theta_1\,(1-\lambda)}{2\theta_4}\, \left(\frac{P_1}{P_1 - \theta_2}\right)\, eP_1 t \tag{48.g}$$

$$r^* = \bar{r}_2 - \frac{\theta_1\,(1-\lambda)}{2\theta_4}\, \left(\frac{P_1}{P_1 - \theta_2}\right)\, eP_1 t \tag{48.h}$$

In the next section we shall make use of the graphs of (48.a)–(48.h)

6   Impact and Dynamic Effects of an Unanticipated Foreign Fiscal Contraction

The decrease in foreign government expenditure will on impact decrease the demand for foreign goods. Since the supply of foreign goods is fixed at any point in time, the real exchange rate will have to appreciate and the foreign real interest rate will have to fall to maintain equilibrium in the foreign goods market, as shown in graphs 3a and 4d. The appreciation of the real exchange rate will reduce the foreign real consumption wage and increase the home real consumption wage, thus creating a real consumption wage differential in favour of the home economy (graph 3b).

Over time this will lead to an inflow of labour to the home economy at the expense of the foreign economy (graph 4a). Therefore the home economy will be operating with an increased labour force and will thus experience a

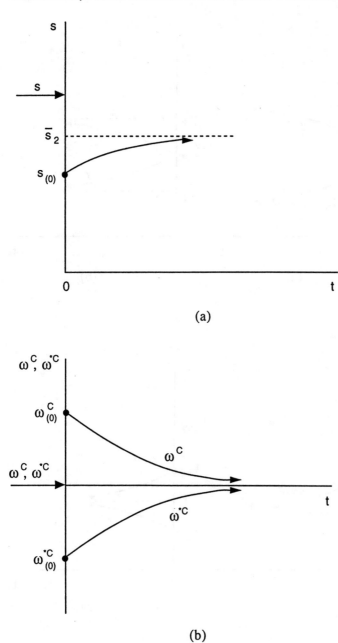

(a)

(b)

Figure 2.3   The dynamics of the real exchange rate and real consumption wages with migration

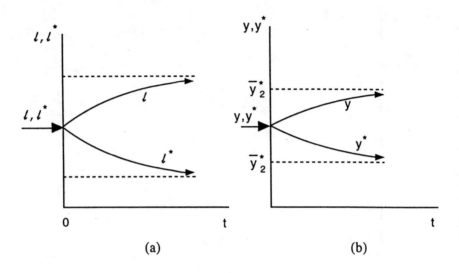

(a)   (b)

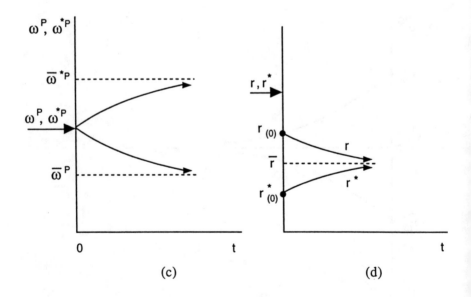

(c)   (d)

Figure 2.4   Paths of adjustment with migration; of foreign and domestic labour force; foreign and domestic output; real product wages and interest rates

rise in output. The foreign economy, being left with a smaller workforce, will experience a loss in output (graph 4b).

The decease (increase) over time in foreign (home) output will require a real exchange rate depreciation and a rise (fall) in the foreign (home) real interest rate to maintain equilibrium in the market for foreign (home) goods. Since in the new steady state the real exchange rate will have to appreciate, this implies that the initial appreciation must exceed the long-run appreciation as shown in graph 3a.

The decrease (increase) over time in foreign (domestic) employment will be followed by a rise (fall) in the foreign (home) real product wage (a movement along the downwards sloping demand for labour), as illustrated in graphs 4a and 4c. In the new steady state the rise (fall) in the foreign (home) real product wage will offset the appreciation of the real exchange rate, leaving the foreign (home) real consumption wage unchanged at its initial steady-state value, as illustrated in graph 3b.

Finally, the behaviour of real interest rates is illustrated in graph 4d. The foreign fiscal contraction decreases the home and the foreign real interest rate in both the short run and long run. However, because over time the supply of foreign (home) goods falls (increases), the foreign (home) interest rate will have to increase (decrease) to maintain equilibrium in the foreign (home) goods markets. Therefore, the foreign interest rate will fall short of its long-run value and the home interest rate will initially exceed its long-run value.

7 The Role of International Migration

To further investigate the role of IML in our results it is both convenient and illuminating to consider first the case of no international migration and then examine how the degree of IML affects the impact and dynamic effects of the unanticipated foreign fiscal contraction. In the context of equations (1)–(11), the case of no international migration can be represented by a situation where workers' behaviour is not influenced by international real wage differentials, i.e. when $z = 0$. With $z = 0$ each country's workforce will be fixed not only in the short run but also over time. As a result, an unanticipated fiscal contraction abroad will have no effect on foreign and domestic employment and thus on foreign and domestic output. However, by creating an excess demand for home goods, it will require a larger long-run real exchange rate appreciation than in the case of IML. Indeed, imposing the condition $z = 0$ and differentiating equations (17), (19) and (20) we obtain

$$\frac{d\bar{S}}{dg^*}\bigg|_{\text{NIML}} = -\frac{1}{2b_1} < 0,$$

while from equation (34) we have

$$\frac{d\bar{S}}{dg^*}\bigg|_{\text{IML}} = -\frac{(1-\varphi)}{2[(1-\lambda)(1+b_3) + b_1(1-\varphi)]} < 0$$

Clearly, the magnitude of the long-run real exchange rate appreciation is larger without international migration than with IML. This is illustrated in Figure 2.5. An unanticipated decrease in foreign government expenditure will cause a long-run fall in the real exchange rate from its initial value S_1 to $S_{2(\text{IML})}$ and $S'_{2(\text{NIML})}$ with and without IML respectively. Since in the latter case there is only one source of dynamics, i.e. the dynamics of the real exchange rate, then, on the assumption that rational agents will not choose an explosive path for the real exchange rate, $\bar{S}'_{2(\text{NIML})}$ will be attained immediately after the unanticipated foreign fiscal contraction, that is, S will jump from $\bar{S}_1$ to $\bar{S}'_{2(\text{NIML})}$. In the case of IML, the new steady-state value of real exchange rate, $S_{2(\text{IML})}$, will be attained over time as indicated by arrow (a).

Assume next the case of a positive and finite degree of IML, i.e. $0 < z < \infty$. How the degree of IML affects the adjustment of the other endogenous variables to the foreign fiscal contraction?

A positive and finite degree of IML will not affect the long-run effects of an unanticipated foreign fiscal contraction, since they are independent of the value of z. However, the degree of IML will affect the paths of the endogenous variables during the transition to the new steady state. Consider the path of the real exchange rate during the transition to long-run equilibrium. It is easy to demonstrate that the short-run effect on the real exchange rate of an unanticipated fiscal contraction abroad will be lower as the degree of IML increases.

Indeed, noting that

$$P_1 P_2 = -2z\,[(1-\varphi)\theta_2 + 2\theta_1(1-\lambda)] \tag{53}$$

$$P_1 + P_2 = \theta_2 - 2z(1-\varphi) \tag{54}$$

and differentiating (53) and (54) with respect to z, we get the expression

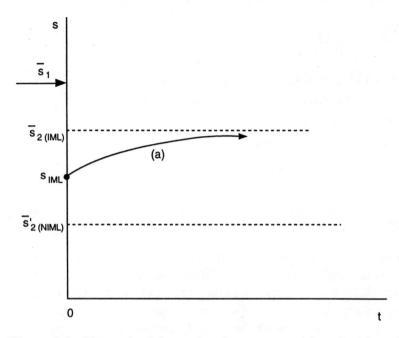

Figure 2.5 The path of the real exchange rate with and without IML

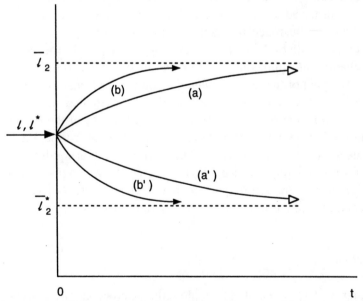

Figure 2.6 The speed of adjustment of home and foreign labour force and the degree of IML

$$\frac{dP_1}{dz} = - \frac{\theta_5}{P_2 - P_1} < 0$$

where $\theta_5 = 2[(1-\varphi)\theta_2 + 2\theta_1(1-\lambda)] - 2(1-\varphi)\rho_1 > 0$.

Differentiating equation (46) with respect to z, we obtain

$$\frac{\partial \left| \frac{dS}{dg*} \right|}{\partial z} = - \frac{(1-\lambda)\theta_1\theta_5}{\theta_4(\rho_2 - \rho_1)(\rho_1 - \theta_2)^2} < 0$$

where

$\left| \dfrac{dS}{dg*} \right|$ is the absolute magnitude of the impact effect on real exchange rate of an unanticipated fiscal contraction abroad.

To illustrate this result consider, first, the paths of ℓ and ℓ^* towards their new long-run values indicated by the pair of arrows (a) and (a′) in Figure 2.6. Let us assume that there is an increase in the degree of IML. A higher degree of IML implies a faster adjustment over time of labour supply in each country towards their new long-run values,[5] and therefore a shorter period of adjustment. In terms of Figure 2.6, the higher degree of IML is represented by the pair of arrows (b) and (b′). Moreover, a faster adjustment of ℓ and ℓ^* will result in a faster adjustment of foreign and home output towards their long-run values, as illustrated in Figure 2.7 by the shorter pair of arrows. Consider, next, the path of the real exchange rate. Let S'_{IML} be the value of the real exchange rate immediately after the unanticipated foreign fiscal contraction. The path of the real exchange rate during the transition to long-run equilibrium is illustrated in Figure 2.8, by the arrow labelled (a). It shows a depreciation over time of the real exchange rate because of the decrease over time in foreign output: as foreign output decreases over time, the real exchange rate has to increase (depreciate) in order to maintain equilibrium in the market for foreign goods. Since a higher degree of IML implies a faster decrease over time in foreign output, the real exchange rate will follow a faster depreciation path, as indicated by the shorter arrow (b).

8   Conclusions

In this chapter we have attempted to explore the macroeconomic aspects of international migration of labour in a two-country model. Our findings can be summarised as follows.

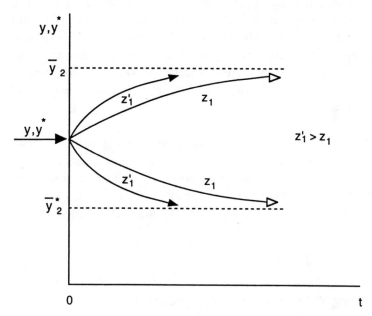

Figure 2.7   The speed of adjustment of home and foreign output and the degree of IML

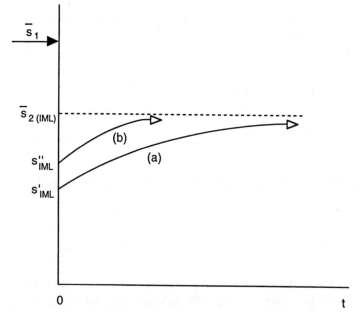

Figure 2.8   Real exchange rate dynamics with IML

1. An unanticipated fiscal contraction abroad will on impact create a real consumption wage differential in favour of the home economy and against the foreign economy. With IML, migration flows over time will eliminate this differential.[6] Moreover, the higher the degree of IML the shorter the period during which the real wage differential between the two countries persists. On the other hand, without IML, real consumption wages will not be equalised.

2. An unanticipated foreign fiscal contraction, by inducing migration flows into the home economy, will increase domestic employment and thus domestic output[7] at the expense of foreign employment and foreign output in the absence of nominal rigidities. Therefore, the home economy will experience over time a cumulative output gain. Indeed, from equation (44) we have

$$\ell^d - \bar{\ell}^d_2 = (\bar{\ell}^d_1 - \bar{\ell}^d_2)\, e^{p_1 t} \qquad (49)$$

Differentiating (49) with respect to time, we obtain

$$\dot{\ell}^d = P_1\,(\ell^d - \bar{\ell}^d_2) \qquad (50.a)$$

Since, for any variable X, we have that $X = \frac{1}{2} X^d$, we may write

$$\dot{\ell} = P_1\,(\ell - \bar{\ell}_2) \qquad (50.b)$$

and using equations (1) and (47), we obtain

$$\dot{y} = - P_1 \left[\frac{(1-\lambda)\varphi}{2\theta_4} \right] e^{p_1 t} \qquad (51)$$

Integrating (51), we obtain the cumulative output gain associated with IML:

$$\int_o^\infty \dot{y}\, dt = \frac{(1-\lambda)\varphi}{2\theta_4} > 0 \qquad (52)$$

Without IML and no nominal rigidities, labour supply in each country will be fixed both in the short run and over time and thus an unanticipated foreign fiscal contraction will have no effect on home output.

3. With or without international migration, an unanticipated decrease in foreign government expenditure will cause an appreciation of the real exchange rate. However, the long-run value of the real exchange rate will be lower without IML.

Notes

1   The unanticipated increase in home government expenditure, by creating an excess demand in the home goods market, will lead to a real exchange rate appreciation and an increase in the interest rates. The increase in interest rates, will reduce the demand for real money balances and the price level in both countries will have to increase to maintain equilibrium in the money markets. The increase in the price level will, in turn, reduce the home and foreign real product wage resulting in higher output supply in each country.

2   We also make the simplifying assumption that workers can move from one country to the other at zero migration costs. The inclusion of a non-zero migration cost does not alter our qualitative results.

3   See, for example, Mortensen (1970) for a detailed analysis.

4   Condition (33) can be explained as follows. First ℓ and ℓ^* are predetermined variables and therefore they can not jump in response to the foreign fiscal contraction. Thus, in deviation form, we have that at time zero, $\ell^W_{(0)} = 0$. Second, since over time we have that

$$\ell = - z(\omega^{*C} - \omega^C) \text{ and } \dot{\ell}^* = - \dot{\ell}$$

we also have that $\dot{\ell}^W = 0$ which means no world flows of labour over time. Since in the short run the world labour force remains unchanged and since there are no world labour flows over time, it follows that $\bar{\ell}^W = \bar{\ell} + \bar{\ell}^* = 0$.

5   Note that

$$\frac{\partial \ell}{\partial z} = - \frac{(1-\lambda) t e^{P_1 t}}{2\theta_4} \frac{d\rho_1}{dz} > 0$$

6   In analysing the effects of IML, some authors, including Quibria (1989) and Rivera-Batiz (1989), claim that migration flows may or may not increase real wages in the country of emigration. In the model we analyse here migration flows will eliminate any real consumption wage differentials.

7   If instead we assume that labour supply in the short run is a negative function of the real exchange rate, then the transmission effects of the unanticipated fiscal contraction abroad on the output will be larger: the real-exchange-rate appreciation not only will induce migration flows over time but will also induce home workers to offer more labour time at home. Since these two effects operate in the same direction, the overall transmission effect on home output will be larger. This case, however, complicates the analysis and this is left for future research.

Appendix

Following e.g. Turnovsky (1986), the solution to (44) is of the following form:

$$\ell^d = \overline{\ell^d}_2 + A\, e^{\rho_1 t} \tag{44.a}$$

$$S = \overline{S}_2 - \frac{\theta_1 A}{\rho_1 - \theta_2}\, e^{\rho_1 t} \tag{44.b}$$

On the assumption that ℓ and ℓ^* move continuously everywhere while S is allowed to jump when an unanticipated shock occurs, it can be shown that the arbitrary constant A is given by

$$-A = d\ell^d = d\overline{\ell} - d\overline{\ell}^* .$$

Since

$$d\overline{\ell} = -d\overline{\ell}^* = \mu_3 \text{ when } dg^* = -1$$

one obtains that

$$A = -\frac{(1-\lambda)}{\theta_4}$$

Substituting the value of A into (45)–(46) we have

$$\ell^d = \ell^d_2 - \frac{(1-\lambda)}{\theta_4}\, e^{\rho_1 t} \tag{45}$$

$$S = \overline{S}_2 + \frac{\theta_1(1-\lambda)}{\theta_4(\rho_1 - \theta_2)}\, e^{\rho_1 t} \tag{46}$$

Since for any variable X we have $\hat{X} = \frac{1}{2}\hat{X}^d$ and $\hat{X}^* = -\frac{1}{2}\hat{X}^d$, using (45), (46) and (1)–(11) we find the paths for all the endogenous variables presented in the main text.

3 International Mobility of Labour, Capital Accumulation and Unanticipated Shocks

1   Introduction

In this chapter we extend our analysis in chapter 1 in two directions. First, we take into account changes over time in the capital stock; and second, we consider the effects of unanticipated non-monetary shocks.

The structure of the chapter is as follows. Section 2 discusses the production side of the economy. As in the previous chapter, the domestic economy is assumed to produce a single good. However, here this single good is not only output available for consumption but also an input for gross capital formation. Also, much of the literature on gross capital formation assumes that labour supply is inelastic. Since our focus is on the macroeconomic effects of international labour mobility (ILM), in this chapter we relax the assumption of an inelastic labour supply in favour of a labour supply depending upon the domestic real wage and foreign real wage.

In section 3, we present the macroeconomic model and examine the adjustment of the domestic economy to an exogenous increase in the demand for real bonds and in the demand for domestic output. We proceed to the analysis of the model in two steps. First, in section 4, we adopt a short-run perspective and ignore changes over time in the capital stock and stock of real bonds. This allows us to gain some insights into the short-run effects of the two shocks on domestic output. Then, in section 5, changes over time in the capital stock and stock of real bonds are taken into account. The impact, dynamic and long-run effects of the two shocks are analysed and the role of ILM in the results is investigated. Finally, section 6 contains concluding comments.

2   The Production Side of the Economy

The model we employ in this chapter is close in spirit to that of Pikoulakis (1981) and Frenkel and Rodriguez (1975) who base their analysis on Uzawa (1969) and Gould (1968).

We assume that the economy under consideration is engaged in two productive activities: the production of output and the production of installed capital. The production of output uses the services of homogeneous labour and homogeneous capital while the production of installed capital requires part of the economy's production. We also assume that output and capital are homogeneous and that the process of installing capital is subject to increasing marginal costs. This, together with the assumption that capital cannot be dismantled once installed, implies that the price of a machine, or equivalently the price of a title to the ownership of a unit of capital, need not equal the price of a unit of output.

A common assumption of much of the literature on capital formation, including Burmeister and Dowell (1970), Chen (1975), Frenkel and Rodriguez (1975), Pikoulakis (1981), Obstfeld and Stockman (1985) and Murphy (1989) is that, at any moment, the available supplies of all factors are inelastically supplied and fully utilised. This means that the quantities of factor services do not vary with changes in factor prices or other shorter-run economic considerations: at any moment, all existing labour or capital offers itself for use regardless of what wage or rental rates prevail. Therefore, factor rewards are determined from demand or productivity considerations. Here we adopt a more general framework of analysis: as in chapter 1 we consider a small open economy with a flexible exchange rate that faces the possibility of a mobile domestic workforce which has two alternatives; i.e. to work in the home market or to work abroad. We thus relax the assumption that labour supply is inelastic in favour of a labour supply function that depends upon two wages: the real domestic wage and the real foreign wage.

Production of Output

As in the previous chapter, we assume a Cobb-Douglas production function:

$$Q = L^\alpha K^{1-\alpha} \qquad (1)$$

where

Q = output

K = capital

L = labour

α = elasticity of output with respect to labour, $0 < \alpha < 1$

Moreover, we have that

$$Q_K (..) = (1-\alpha) (\frac{L}{K})^\alpha > 0 \text{ for } 0 \leqslant K < \infty$$

$$Q_K (..) \to 0 \text{ as } \frac{L}{K} \to 0$$

$$Q_K (..) \to \infty \text{ as } \frac{L}{K} \to \infty$$

$$Q_{KK} = - \alpha(1-\alpha) L^\alpha K^{-(1+\alpha)} < 0 \text{ for } 0 \leqslant K < \infty$$

Production of Installed Capital

The economy is engaged in the production of installed capital to meet its own demand for gross capital formation. Along the lines suggested by Pikoulakis (1981) and Frenkel and Rodriguez (1975), we assume that installed capital is produced by output and that the production function, which generates installed capital, has constant returns to scale. The process of transforming output into capital is costly, and this calls for a distinction between investment and gross capital formation. Specifically, we assume that

$$G = G(I) \tag{2}$$

with

$$G(0) = 0, G'(.) > 0, G'(0) = 1, G''(.) < 0$$

where

$G \equiv \dot{K} + \delta K$ = gross capital formation

$\dot{K} = \dfrac{dK}{dt}$

δ = the percentage rate of capital depreciation, a constant

I = the units of output used in the production of G units of installed capital

One may invert (2) to get investment, I, as a function of gross capital formation:

$$I = H(G) \tag{3}$$

with

$$H(0) = 0, H'(.) = \frac{1}{G'(.)} > o, H'(0) = 1$$

and

$$H''(.) = -\frac{G''(.)H'(.)}{[G'(.)]^2} > 0$$

Equation, (3) states that the process of gross capital formation involves increasing marginal costs, measured in output units. The relationships implied by (2) and (3) are illustrated in Figures 3.1 and 3.2.

In what follows we take the investment function (the cost of adjustment function) to be a quadratic function given by[1]

$$I = H(G) = G + G^2 \tag{3'}$$

The Market for the Services of the Factors of Production

To ensure perfect competition and full employment of factors of production, much of the literature on capital formation makes the following four assumptions:

i) the two types of services, capital services and labour services, are homogeneous in themselves (each one in itself);

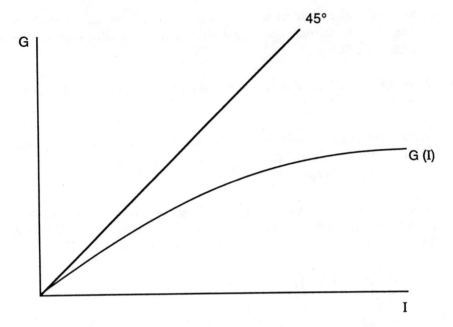

Figure 3.1   Gross capital formation

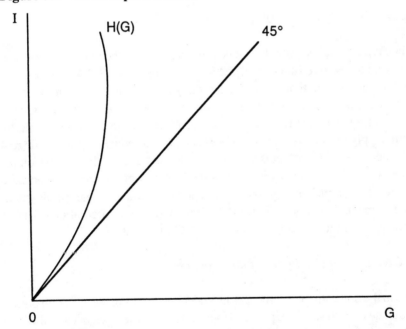

Figure 3.2   Investment

ii) the supply of each of these services is completely inelastic. Hence, the wage rate and the rental on capital adjust to maintain full employment in each of the factor markets;

iii) the services of capital are proportional to the stock of capital used in the production;

iv) for every unit of capital there corresponds a claim to the ownership of that unit. Thus the claims of ownership issued, to be called equities, are identically equal to the units of capital.

Here we relax the assumption of inelastic labour supply and assume a labour supply function that depends on both the domestic wage and the foreign wage. Like in chapter 1, we assume that labour supply takes the form

$$L^S = \left(\frac{W}{P} \right)^{C_1} S^{-C_3} \tag{4}$$

where $S = \dfrac{EP'^*}{P}$ is the real exchange rate

and $C_3 = (1-\lambda)C_1 + \lambda C_2 > 0$.

As in chapter 1, labour supply is a positive function of the real product wage, $\frac{W}{P}$, and a negative function of the real exchange rate, S. We may, briefly, recall our analysis in that chapter: other things being equal, an increase in the real product wage induces home residents to increase their work-time. On the other hand, an increase in S, a real exchange rate depreciation, reduces domestic labour supply through two distinct channels. First, it reduces the domestic real consumer wage. This effect is captured by the first term in the expression for C_3, i.e. $-(1-\lambda)C_1$. Second, by increasing the foreign wage in terms of domestic currency units, it makes employment abroad more attractive than employment in the home and economy. This effect, which is due to international labour mobility, is captured by the second term in C_3, i.e. $(-\lambda C_2)$.

The Optimisation Conditions of the Economy

Firms in the domestic economy operate under conditions of perfect competition and pursue maximisation of profits. Households own the stock of capital which they rent to firms, and, for every unit of capital, there corresponds a claim to the ownership of that unit. Thus, the claims of ownership issued, to be called equities, are identically equal to the units of capital.

The firms' revenues are composed of sales of output net of investment, that is $L^\alpha K^{1-\alpha}$ - I, and of sales of new shares resulting from new capital formation, that is $P_K \dot{K}$. The firms' payments are composed of wages, i.e. ωL, and the rental on capital $r_K K$. Therefore, profits are given by

$$\pi = L^\alpha K^{1-\alpha} - H(G) + P_K \dot{K} - \omega L - r_K K \qquad (5)$$

where

P_K : the price of an equity, in terms of output

$\omega = \dfrac{W}{P}$: the real product wage rate

r_K : the net rental on capital net of capital maintenance, measured in units of domestic output

The first-order conditions for a maximum of (5) are:

$$\omega = \alpha \left(\frac{K}{L} \right)^{1-\alpha} \qquad (5.1)$$

$$r_K = (1-\alpha) \left(\frac{K}{L} \right)^{-\alpha} - H'(.)\delta \qquad (5.2)$$

$$P_K = H'(.) \qquad (5.3)$$

To derive a demand-for-labour function one may use (5.1) and the definition of ω:

$$L^d = K \left(\frac{1}{\alpha} \right)^{\frac{1}{1-\alpha}} \left(\frac{W}{P} \right)^{-\frac{1}{1-\alpha}} \qquad (6)$$

Equilibrium in the labour market requires that $L^d = L^s$. Solving (4') and (6) for ω and L, one obtains

$$\omega = \alpha^{\Psi_1} S^{\Psi_2 C_3} K^{\Psi_2} \qquad (7)$$

$$L = \alpha^{C_1 \Psi_1} S^{-\Psi_1 C_3} K^{\Psi_2 C_1} \qquad (8)$$

Substituting (8) into the production function we obtain an expression for the aggregate supply of domestic output:

$$Q = \mu_0 S^{-\alpha \Psi_1 C_3} K^{(1+C_1)\Psi_2} \tag{9}$$

where

$$\mu_0 = \alpha^{\alpha C_1 \Psi_1} > 0$$

$$\Psi_1 = \frac{1}{1+C_1(1-\alpha)} > 0$$

$$\Psi_2 = (1-\alpha)\,\Psi_1 > 0$$

The effect of a change in S on domestic output is

$$Q_S = -\mu_1 C_3 S^{-(1+\alpha C_3 \Psi_1)} K^{(1+C_1)\Psi_2} < 0 \tag{9.a}$$

where

$$\mu_1 = \mu_0 \,\alpha\, \Psi_1 > 0$$

That is, an increase in S, reduces domestic labour supply and thus domestic output. The effect of a change in the capital stock on domestic output is

$$Q_K = \mu_2 S^{-\alpha \Psi_1 C_3} K^{-\alpha \Psi_1} > 0 \tag{9.b}$$

$$\mu_2 = \mu_0 (1+C_1)\,\Psi_2 > 0$$

Aggregate Investment and the Evolution of Capital

The third equation in the set of the first-order conditions (5.1)–(5.3) is

$$P_K = H'(.) \tag{5.3}$$

This equation states that the marginal cost of installing capital, measured in output units equals the market price of capital, P_K. Inverting (5.3), we get

$$G \equiv \dot{K} + \delta K = h(P_K) \tag{10}$$

$$h'(P_K) = \frac{1}{H''(.)} > 0, \, h(1) = 0$$

Assuming no population growth, we can rewrite (10) as

$$\dot{K} = h(P_K) - \delta K \tag{11}$$

Equation (11) describes the evolution of the capital stock. We also have

$$I = H(G) = H(h(P_K)) = I(P_K) \tag{12}$$

$$I'(P_K) = \frac{H'(.)}{H''(.)} > 0, \, I(1) = 0$$

Equation (12) describes the demand for output as an input in gross capital formation. Since it is assumed that

$$I = H(G) = G + G^2,$$

we have

$$H'(.) = 1 + 2G \text{ and } H'' = 2$$

Thus

$$h'(P_K) = \frac{1}{2}, \, I'(P_K) = \frac{1}{2} + G$$

Setting $\dot{K} = 0$ in (11), we obtain a locus showing combinations of P_K and K for which the capital stock remains unchanged. This locus is shown in Figure 3.3.

The slope of the $\dot{K} = 0$ locus is positive.

$$\frac{\delta}{h'(P_K)} = 2\delta > 0,$$

reflecting the assumption of a quadratic investment function. At the point where $P_K = 1$, gross capital formation is zero. As K rises, gross capital formation rises, raising the marginal cost of installing capital. This increases P_K and thus the profitability of capital, so that the production of installed capital is itself increased.

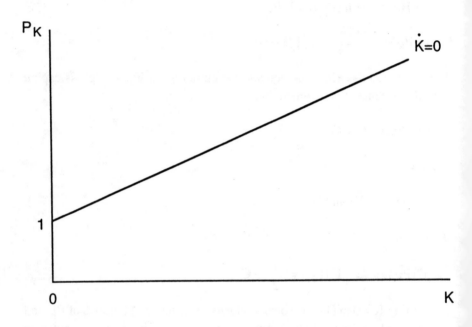

Figure 3.3   The $\dot{K} = 0$ locus shows combination of P_K and K for which the capital stock remains unchanged

3   The Macroeconomic Model

The domestic economy can be described by the following set of equations:

$$\frac{M}{P} = L\,(Q\,(S,K)), \qquad\qquad L\,(.) > 0 \qquad\qquad\qquad (13)$$

$$B = F(\rho,\rho^*)\,w + U_1, \qquad\qquad F_1 < 0,\, F_2 > 0 \qquad\qquad (14)$$

$$w = B + P_K\,K \qquad\qquad\qquad\qquad\qquad\qquad\qquad (14.1)$$

$$\rho = \frac{r_K K}{P_K K} + \frac{\dot{P}_K{}^e}{P_K} = \frac{Q_K}{P_K} - \delta + \frac{\dot{P}_K{}^e}{P_K} \qquad\qquad (15)$$

$$Q\,(S,K) - I(P_K) = D\,(Q(S,K)) + X(S) + U_2 \qquad\qquad (16)$$

$$X'(.) > 0,\, D' > 0,\, 0 < D' < 1,\, I'(.) > 0$$

where

M is the money stock
w is real wealth
ρ is the market rate of return on domestic equity
B is the number of claims by residents on nonresidents
ρ^* is the market rate of return on B
U_1 is a shift variable in the bond demand function
U_2 is a shift variable in the aggregate demand function

The short-run equilibrium of the model is described by equations (13) to (16). Equation (13) is the money-market equilibrium condition. Equation (14) describes the demand for bonds. We assume that non-monetary wealth, w, consists of the market value of the entire stock of capital (held in the form of equity by domestic residents alone) and claims on nonresidents. These claims on non-residents, B, are assumed to be real bonds expressed and denominated in units of the domestic consumption goods.

Equation (15) is the definition of the domestic real interest rate, while equation (16) describes equilibrium in the market for the home produced goods.

In equation (13) we assume a quantity theory of money, i.e. real money balances depend positively on the volume of transactions proxied by domestic output. In equation (14) we adopt a portfolio-balance approach to model claims abroad. Accordingly, the part of non-monetary wealth held in the form of these claims is a decreasing function of the market rate of return on equities, ρ, and an increasing function of its own market rate of return ρ^*. By assumption ρ^* is exogenous. In equation (15), the domestic real interest rate is the sum of two components: the rental component and the capital-gain component. The rental component is the ratio of the rental income on domestic capital, $r_K K$ to the market value of this capital, $P_K K$.

The left-hand side of (16) gives the supply of domestic output available for consumption, while the right-hand side gives the demand for domestic output for consumption purposes. Since the left-hand side of this equation has already been analysed in section 2, we focus our attention on the right-hand side. Aggregate demand consists of two components: total domestic consumption D(..), and net exports demand X(.) . Total domestic consumption is taken to depend positively on the domestic output. Net exports demand are taken to be an increasing function of the real exchange rate.

At any point in time K and B are predetermined: the stock of real bonds can change only over time through current account imbalances and the stock of capital changes only over time through investment. In addition, M is policy determined.

Therefore, given expectations, there are four equations in four unknowns: P, P_K, S, ρ.

Over time the evolution of capital, is given by

$$\dot{K} = h\,(P_K) - \delta K \tag{17}$$

The current account can be described by

$$\dot{B} = X(S) \tag{18}$$

The third dynamic equation describes the evolution of P_K and is given by equation (15) which we rewrite here as

$$\dot{P}_K{}^e = (\rho + \delta)\,P_K - Q_K\,(S, K) \tag{19}$$

Therefore, as the economy moves from one steady-state to another, there are six equations to be considered i.e. (13)–(14) and (16)–(19) in six endogenous variables: P, P_K, S, ρ, K, B.

4 Short-run Effects of Unanticipated Shocks under Static Expectations

To gain insights into the impact effects of changes in U_1 and U_2, here we assume static expectations and ignore changes over time in K and B.

Solving equations (13)–(16) for the impact effects of U_1 and U_2 shocks on P_K, S and ρ we find the results reported in Table 3.1 (algebraic expressions for the impact effects are given in Appendix 1).

Table 3.1   Impact effects of U_1 and U_2 on P_K, S and ρ

	U_1	U_2
P_K	-	+
S	+	-
ρ	+	+

An exogenous increase in the demand for real bonds ($dU_1 > 0$) lowers the market price of capital and increases the real exchange rate and the domestic interest rate. On the other hand, an exogenous increase in the demand for home goods increases the market price of capital and the domestic interest rate and appreciates the real exchange rate.

An analysis of our findings is in order. To facilitate the analysis we make use of three figures each one corresponding to each of equations (14), (15) and (16), i.e. the market for real bonds, the definition of the real domestic interest rate, and the market for home goods. Each figure is drawn in the (P_K, S) space for given short-run values of K, B and ρ.

The BB schedule in Figure 3.4 describes the real bond market and is horizontal in the (P_K, S) space. In the short run, the stock of capital and the stock of real bonds are given. Hence, the BB locus depends only on the market price of capital, P_K. A shift of the BB locus upwards, (downwards) is associated with a rise (fall) in the real interest rate. To show this we consider a rise (fall) in ρ. This rise (fall) in ρ will decrease (increase) the demand for real bonds requiring a rise (fall) in P_K. The rise (fall) in P_K, by increasing (reducing) real wealth, will achieve equilibrium in the market for real bonds.

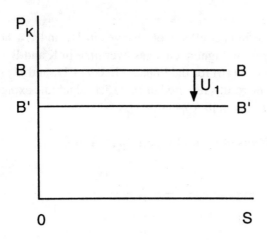

Figure 3.4   The BB schedule: the real bond market

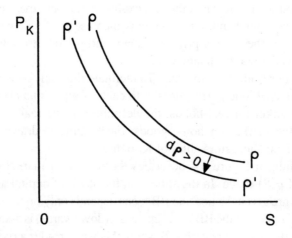

Figure 3.5   The $\rho\rho$ locus: combinations of P_K and S which keep the real interest rate unchanged

The $\rho\rho$ locus in Figure 3.5 shows combinations of P_K and S which keep the real interest rate, ρ, unchanged. Along this locus P_K and S are negatively related. As is apparent from the definition of ρ an increase in S reduces the marginal productivity of capital since $Q_{KS}(..) < 0$. Indeed, as we have already mentioned in section 2, an increase in S has two effects: it reduces the domestic supply of labour by lowering the domestic real consumer wage; and it induces home residents to undertake more work abroad. Therefore, an increase in S leaves domestic capital with less labour to work with and the marginal productivity of capital falls. If ρ is to remain unchanged, a fall in P_K is required. A shift of the $\rho\rho$ locus to the left is associated with an increase in ρ. This is because an increase in ρ, for any given P_K, can be achieved with a higher productivity of capital, which in turn requires more labour for capital to work with. This is possible only through a fall in S. The GG locus in Figure 3.6 shows combinations of P_K and S which maintain equilibrium in the goods market. This locus has a negative slope. To explain why this is so, consider a fall in the real exchange rate. The fall in S will create two effects: first, it will increase domestic employment and thus domestic output; and second it will lead to a fall in net exports due to reduced competitiveness. The overall effect of the fall in S will be an excess supply of domestic goods. Equilibrium in the market for home good can be maintained through a rise in the market price of capital, P_K. The rise in P_K will increase investment, i.e. more units of output will be used for capital formation. This will eliminate the excess supply of output and hence will restore equilibrium in the domestic goods market. An exogenous increase in the demand for home goods ($dU_2 > 0$) will shift the GG-locus to the left: given P_K, it will increase the demand for home goods and this will require a fall in S to restore equilibrium.[2] We may now put all pieces together as shown in Figure 3.7.

The GG locus in Figure 3.7 is taken to be steeper than the locus, since we make the plausible assumption that a change in S will lead to a larger change in P_K in the goods market rather than the one required by the definition of the real interest rate. This corresponds to the condition

$$Q_{KS}\,\theta'_2 - Q_K < 0 \qquad\qquad (20)$$

where

$$\theta'_2 = \frac{I'(.)}{(1-D')\,Q_S - X'(.)} < 0,$$

We may now turn our attention to the effects of the two exogenous shocks.

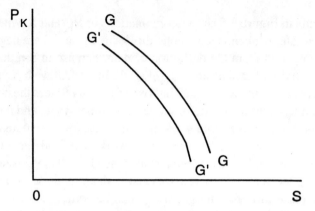

Figure 3.6   The GG locus: combinations of P_K and S which maintain equilibrium in the goods market

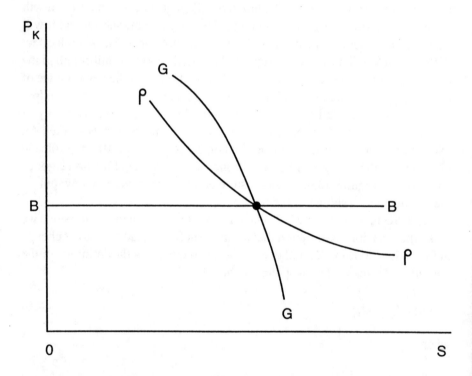

Figure 3.7   Equilibrium in the real interest rate and the markets for goods and real bonds

An Exogenous Increase in U_1

As we show in Figure 3.8, an increase in the demand for real bonds, $dU_1 > 0$, is represented by the downwards shift of the B_1B_1 locus to B_2B_2. That is, an increase in U_1 will create an excess demand for real bonds. Equilibrium in the asset market will require a fall in real wealth which can only be achieved in the short run through a fall in P_K.

In the goods market, the fall in P_K, by reducing investment, will create excess supply. Hence equilibrium in this market will require a rise in the real exchange rate. This is represented by point B on GG locus.

From the definition of the real interest rate, the rise in S and the fall in P_K will shift the $\rho_1\rho_1$ locus leftwards to $\rho_2\rho_2$: first the rise in S, by reducing domestic employment, will leave capital with less labour to work with and thus the marginal productivity of capital will fall. On the other hand, the fall in P_K increases ρ. Overall, the fall in P_K and the rise in S will lead to a rise in the real interest rate which, as we have seen in Figure 3.5, will shift $\rho_1\rho_1$ locus leftwards to $\rho_2\rho_2$. Moreover, the rise in ρ will shift the B_2B_2 locus, upwards to B_3B_3. The point of new equilibrium is C where P_K is lower while ρ and S are higher than their initial values.

An Exogenous Increase in U_2

In Figure 3.9, an exogenous increase in U_2 will increase the demand for domestic output. Equilibrium in the domestic goods market will thus require a fall in S: the fall in S will stimulate production and will reduce net exports. Thus, following the increase in U_2, the G_1G_1 locus will shift to the left along the B_1B_1 locus.

From the definition of the real interest rate, the fall in S will serve to increase ρ. This is represented by the leftward shift of the $\rho_1\rho_1$ locus to $\rho_2\rho_2$, along the B_1B_1 locus.

Finally, the resulting increase in ρ will affect the B_1B_1 locus, shifting it upwards. The new equilibrium is represented by point C, where P_K and ρ are higher and S is lower than their initial equilibrium values.

Impact Effects on Output

Because output in the short run simply depends on the value of the real exchange rate, the impact effects on domestic production are linked with the impact effects on the real exchange rate.[3] An exogenous increase in the demand

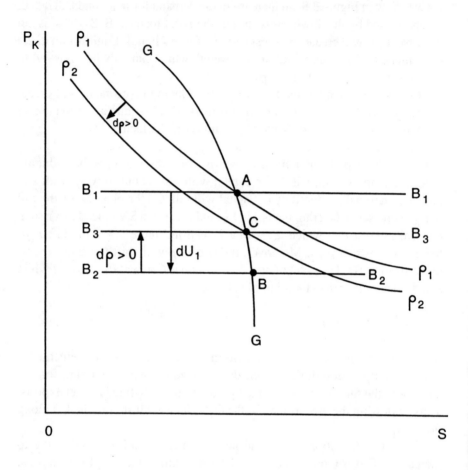

Figure 3.8   **Equilibrium in the real interest rate and the markets for goods and real bonds under an exogenous increase in the demand for real bonds**

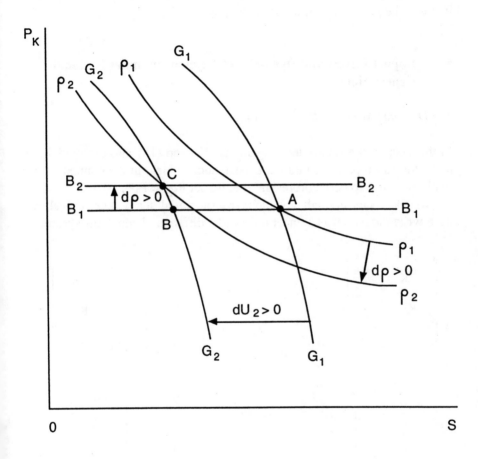

Figure 3.9 **Equilibrium in the real interest rate and the markets for goods and real bonds under an exogenous increase in the demand for domestic output**

for real bonds ($dU_1 > 0$) will create a real exchange rate depreciation and, by reducing domestic employment, will lead to a fall in domestic output. By contrast, an exogenous increase in aggregate demand ($dU_2 > 0$) will create a real exchange rate appreciation, which, by increasing employment, will increase the production of domestic output.

5   Impact Effects and Dynamics of Adjustment under Rational Expectations

The Dynamic Model in Reduced Form

In this section we reintroduce equations (17) and (18) into the model and make the assumption of rational expectations, which, in the context of our model amounts to perfect foresight (i.e. we set $\dot{P}_K{}^e = \dot{P}_K$).

We also focus on small deviations from an initial steady state. This allows us to write the model as a linear third-order differential equations system:

$$
\begin{bmatrix} \hat{\dot{P}}_K \\ \hat{\dot{K}} \\ \hat{\dot{B}} \end{bmatrix} = \begin{bmatrix} V_3 & -V_2 & V_1 \\ \frac{1}{2} & -\delta & 0 \\ \sigma_2 & -\sigma_1 & 0 \end{bmatrix} \begin{bmatrix} \hat{P}_K \\ \hat{K} \\ \hat{B} \end{bmatrix} +
$$

$$
+ \begin{bmatrix} -\dfrac{\overline{P}_K}{F_1\overline{W}} & -\dfrac{Z_4}{\theta_1} & 0 \\ 0 & 0 & 0 \\ 0 & \dfrac{X'(.)}{\theta_1} & 0 \end{bmatrix} \begin{bmatrix} du_1 \\ du_2 \\ 0 \end{bmatrix} \qquad (22)
$$

where

$$
V_1 = \frac{\overline{P}_K[1-F(..)]}{F_1\overline{W}} < 0
$$

$$V_2 = Z_3 - Z_4 \theta'_3 < 0$$

$$V_3 = Z_2 - Z_4 \theta'_2 \lessgtr 0$$

$$Z_2 = \frac{Q_K}{\overline{P}_K} - \frac{\overline{P}_K F(..)}{\overline{w}F_1} > 0$$

$$Z_3 = Q_{KK} + \frac{\overline{P}_K{}^2 F(..)}{\overline{w}F_1} < 0$$

$$Z_4 = Q_{KS} < 0, \qquad\qquad\qquad \theta_2 = I'(.) > 0$$

$$\sigma_1 = X'(.) \, \theta'_3 < 0, \qquad\qquad \theta_3 = (1-D')Q_K > 0$$

$$\sigma_2 = X'(.) \, \theta'_2 < 0$$

$$\theta'_2 = \frac{I'(.)}{(1-D')Q_s - X'(.)} < 0$$

$$\theta'_3 = \frac{(1-D')Q_K}{(1-D')Q_s - X'(.)} < 0$$

We turn now to an intuitive explanation of the V_is and σ_is. The effect on $P_K{}^e$ of a change in B is captured by the parameter V_1. An increase in B will increase the supply of real bonds, thus requiring a fall in ρ to maintain equilibrium in the real bonds market. The fall in ρ will in turn require a fall in expected capital gains.

The effect on $P_K{}^e$ of a change in K is captured by the parameter $-V_2 > 0$. An increase in K will decrease the marginal productivity of capital so that given ρ, $P_K{}^e$ will increase. The increase in K also increases real wealth, thus causing ρ to rise. This requires a further increase in $P_K{}^e$, given the definition of ρ. Both effects are captured by the first term in the expression for $-V_2$, i.e. $-Z_3 > 0$. In addition to these effects, the increase in K also increases S: the rise in K increases domestic output supply and equilibrium in the domestic goods market requires a real exchange rate appreciation. The appreciation reduces further the marginal productivity of capital, so an increase in $P_K{}^e$ is required to keep ρ unchanged. This effect is captured by the second term in the expression for $-V_2$, i.e. $Z_4 \, \theta'_3 > 0$.

The effect on $\dot{P}_K{}^e$ of a change in P_K is captured by the parameter V_3. An increase in P_K will increase, given ρ, expected capital gains. This increase in P_K will also increase real wealth, thus requiring a rise in ρ to maintain equilibrium in the bonds market. This will in turn require an increase in expected capital gains. This effect is positive and is captured by the parameter Z_2 which is the first component of V_3. In addition to this effect, an increase in P_K will also cause an appreciation of the real exchange rate. This is because an increase in P_K increases investment but a higher rate of investment can be sustained only through higher production and thus through a lower real exchange rate. Since any fall in S increases domestic labour supply, the appreciation of the real exchange rate will in turn increase the marginal productivity of capital. The increase in the marginal productivity of capital, however, requires a fall in expected capital gains to keep the real interest rate unchanged. Thus, the second effect on $\dot{P}_K{}^e$ of a change in P_K, captured by $-Z_4\,\theta'_2$, is negative. However, under the assumption of a high degree of asset substitutability, on balance the positive effect can be taken to lead to a rise in expected capital gains.

The effect on $\dot{B}$ of a change in P_K is captured by the parameter σ_2: an increase in P_K increases investment and this requires a real exchange rate appreciation to maintain equilibrium in the goods market. The appreciation of the real exchange rate, in turn creates a current account deficit and this reduces overtime the stock of real bonds, i.e. $\sigma_2 < 0$. By contrast, an increase in K will increase the supply of output, thus requiring a real exchange rate depreciation to maintain equilibrium in the goods market. The depreciation of real exchange rate will in turn increase the stock of real bonds i.e. $-\sigma_1 > 0$.

Stability Conditions

The characteristic equation of (22) is

$$\mu^3 - (V_3 - \delta)\mu^2 + (\tfrac{1}{2}V_2 - \delta V_3 - \sigma_2 V_1)\mu - [V_1(\delta\sigma_2 - \tfrac{1}{2}\sigma_1)] = 0 \qquad (23)$$

In systems like the one described by (22) we expect two negative roots (associated with the predetermined variables K and B) and one positive root (associated with the non-predetermined variable P_K). The necessary condition for this to be the case is that the constant term in (23) (which equals $-(\mu_1\mu_2\mu_3)$) is negative. This requirement imposes the stability condition

$$2\delta > \frac{\sigma_1}{\sigma_2} > 0 \tag{24}$$

The sufficient condition, which requires a negative coefficient of μ, is satisfied given the assumption of high substitutability between bonds and domestic equities and thus the sign of V_3. This suggests that (22) has two negative roots and one positive root.

We now turn our attention to the economic meaning of the stability condition (24). In section 1 we assumed a quadratic investment function given by equation (3'). Given equations (10) and (12) we may write

$$h'(P_K) = \frac{1}{H''(.)} = \tfrac{1}{2} > 0$$

and

$$I'(P_K) = \frac{H'(.)}{H''(.)} = \frac{H'(.)}{2} > 0$$

Therefore, upon substitution, one may write the stability condition as

$$\delta H'(G) > (1-D')Q_K \tag{25}$$

where D' is the marginal propensity to consume.

To explain the stability condition let us consider a rise in K from its initial equilibrium value. Such a rise in K will increase both the supply and the demand for domestic output. The net increase in domestic output is captured by the right hand side of (25). However, an increase in capital is possible only through the process of transforming units of output into installed capital. This process is costly and can be achieved at an additional cost equal to $H'(G)$, i.e. the marginal cost of installing capital measured in units of output. Also, for any additional unit of capital, gross capital formation increases by δ. Hence, any rise in K creates an additional maintenance cost which is reflected in the left-hand side of (25). The stability condition guarantees that starting from an equilibrium position, any further rise in K creates a maintenance cost that exceeds the net benefit in terms of output so it will be unprofitable for the economy to expand capital formation.

Next we turn to the derivation of an algebraic expression for the stable path. Assuming unique stability and omitting here the steps involved in deriving the unique stable path, we report the solution for this path:[4]

$$\hat{P}_K = \{ \ell_2 \hat{K} + \ell_3 \hat{B} \} / \ell_1 \tag{26}$$

where

$$\ell_1 = - V_1 \sigma_1 \sigma_2 + V_2 \sigma_2 [V_3 - (\rho_1 + \rho_2)] - \sigma_1 (\rho_1 - V_2)(\rho_2 - V_3) > 0$$

$$\ell_2 = V_2{}^2 \sigma_2 - \sigma_1{}^2 V_1 - \sigma_1 V_2 V_3 \gtreqless 0$$

$$\ell_3 = - \{ V_1 V_2 \sigma_2 + \sigma_1 V_1 [\rho_1 + \rho_2 - V_3] + V_2 \rho_1 \rho_2 \} > 0$$

Under the assumption of high substitutability between real bonds and domestic equities, we may take the sign of ℓ_2 to be negative: V_1 is small and σ_1 is less than one, so that the second term in ℓ_2 is negligible.

5.3   Long-run Effects of Unanticipated Changes in the Shift Variables U_1 and U_2

Steady-state equilibrium requires that $\dot{B} = \dot{K} = \dot{P}_K = 0$. Imposing these conditions, we obtain from (22)

$$V_1 \, dB + Z_2 dP_K - Z_3 dK = \frac{\overline{P}_K}{F_1 \overline{w}} \, dU_1 \tag{27}$$

$$\tfrac{1}{2} \, dP_K - \delta d\overline{K} = 0 \tag{28}$$

$$\theta_2 \, dP_K - \theta_3 d_K = - \, dU_2 \tag{29}$$

Solving (27)–(29) and using the resulting expressions for K, P_K and B, we can find the long-run effects on real exchange rate, real interest rate, domestic employment and domestic output. We report our findings in Table 3.2.

The expression $(\theta_3 - 2\delta\theta_2)$ is negative from the stability condition while σ_0, the elasticity of domestic employment with respect to the stock of capital,[5] is also positive since a higher stock of capital is associated with higher domestic employment.

To explain these results we shall make use of two figures: the first depicts the $\dot{K} = 0$ and $\dot{B} = 0$ loci; the second shows equilibrium in the real bonds market, for any given P_K and K.

In Figure 3.10 the $\dot{K} = 0$ locus describes the evolution of capital and the

Table 3.2   Long-run effects of U_1 and U_2 on K, P_K, B, ρ, S, ℓ and Q

	dU_1	dU_2
$d\bar{K}$	0	$\dfrac{1}{\theta_3 - 2\delta\theta_2} < 0$
$d\bar{P}_K$	0	$\dfrac{2\delta}{\theta_3 - 2\delta\theta_2} < 0$
$d\bar{B}$	$\dfrac{1}{1-F(..)} > 0$	$\dfrac{Z_3 - 2\delta Z_2}{V_1(\theta_3 - 2\delta\theta_2)} < 0$
$d\bar{\rho}$	0	$\dfrac{\bar{P}_K Q_{KK} - 2\delta Q_K}{(\theta_3 - 2\delta\theta_2)(\bar{P}_K)^2} > 0$
$d\bar{S}$	0	0
$d\bar{\ell}$	0	$\dfrac{\sigma_0}{\theta_3 - 2\delta\theta_2} < 0$
$d\bar{Q}$	0	$\dfrac{Q_K}{\theta_3 - 2\delta\theta_2} < 0$

$\dot{B} = 0$ locus describes the evolution of the stock of real bonds. Since we have analysed the $\dot{K} = 0$ locus in section 2, we shall focus our attention on the $\dot{B} = 0$ locus. As equation (18) suggests, changes in the stock of real bonds can only occur through current account imbalances and hence through changes in the real exchange rate. Therefore, the $\dot{B} = 0$ locus represents combinations of P_K and K which sustain an unchanged real exchange rate. The $\dot{B}$ locus is upward sloping, since an increase in K will increase the supply of output and this will require an increase in P_K to maintain equilibrium in the goods market at an unchanged real exchange rate.

The two loci intersect each other at point A. The stability condition, equation (24), requires that the $\dot{K} = 0$ locus is steeper than the $\dot{B} = 0$ locus.

Changes in U_1 have no impact on the position of the two loci and thus in the long-run values of P_K and K. However, an increase in U_2 shifts the $\dot{B} = 0$

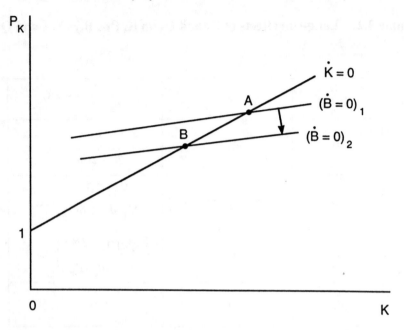

Figure 3.10 The capital stock and the price of capital under rational expectations in the case of the two unanticipated shocks

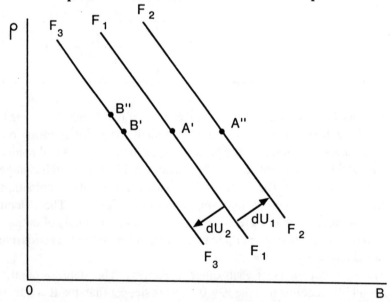

Figure 3.11 The real interest rate and the stock of foreign bonds in the case of the two unanticipated shocks

locus to the right, since, for any given P_K, a higher K is required to keep the stock of real bonds unchanged. Hence, an increase in U_2 leads to a new long-run equilibrium at point B, where both P_K and K are lower than their initial values.

We turn now to an intuitive explanation of these results. An increase in U_1 increases the demand for real bonds. Equilibrium in the real bond market requires either an increase in the long-run stock of bonds $\overline{B}$, or a decrease in real wealth through a fall in the long-run values of P_K and K. However, the changes in P_K and K required to maintain equilibrium in the real bond market will result in changes in the long-run value of real exchange rate $\overline{S}$. But in the new steady-state $\dot{B} = 0$, and this requires the long-run real exchange rate to remain unchanged. Therefore, only an increase in the long-run stock of real bonds will maintain equilibrium in the asset market, following an increase in U_1.

In terms of Figure 3.11, the F_1F_1 curve shifts to the right and the point of new steady-state equilibrium is A″. Since the long-run values of P_K, K and S are unaffected by an increase in U_1, the real interest rate, domestic employment and domestic output will be unaffected too.

On the other hand, an increase in U_2 leads to a crowding out of investment and thus to a reduction in the steady-state level of capital stock. An increase in U_2 increases the demand for domestic output. Equilibrium in the goods market requires a lower market price of capital at given K, i.e. a lower P_K, by reducing investment, will increase the domestic output being available for consumption. This is represented in Figure 3.10 by the shift of the $\dot{B} = 0$ locus to the right, along the $\dot{K} = 0$ locus. The lower market price of capital, however, also leads to a lower long-run stock of capital stock, since P_K and K are forced to move in the same direction by the $\dot{K} = 0$ locus.

The new steady-state equilibrium will be at point B, where both P_K and K are smaller than at point A.

The fall in the long-run values of K and P_K, by reducing real wealth, will in turn lead to a fall in the long-run stock of real bonds, given ρ. In terms of Figure 3.11, this is represented by the shift of F_1F_1 leftwards to F_3F_3, (point B′). Moreover, the fall in K and P_K increases the real domestic interest rate (the opportunity cost of holding real bonds) and this leads to a further decrease in the long-run stock of real bonds, i.e. an upward movement along the F_3F_3 curve, (point B″).

Finally, in the new steady-state equilibrium, the economy will be left with less capital and, therefore, domestic employment and output will be lower than their initial steady-state values.

That a positive demand shock leads to a long-run fall in the capital stock and hence in output may seem counter intuitive but it can be justified on the basis of the stability condition $(1-D')Q_K - 2\delta I'(.) < 0$. As we mentioned in section 5.2, this condition implies that starting from an equilibrium position, any further increases in K create a maintenance cost that exceeds the net benefit in terms of higher output so that it will be unprofitable for the economy to expand capital formation. Indeed, differentiation of the long-run version of the goods market equilibrium condition (16) yields the equation

$$[(1-D')Q_K - 2\delta I'(.)] \, dK = dU_2 \qquad\qquad (29.a)$$

Equation (29.a) says that as long as the stability condition $(1-D')Q_K - 2\delta I'(.) < 0$ is satisfied, the goods market can be brought back to equilibrium following a positive demand shock only through a fall in the capital stock.

At this point it should be noted that since international labour mobility is simply generated by changes in the real exchange rate and since S remains unchanged from one steady state to another, the presence of ILM has no impact on the long-run properties of the model.

Impact and Dynamic Effects of Changes in U_1 and U_2

Having analysed the stability condition and the long-run properties of the model, we can now proceed to examine the impact and dynamic effects of the two shocks. To derive algebraic expressions for the impact effects we make use of the stable path of the economy given by equation (26). However, while the impact effects of changes in U_1 are clear in their signs, the impact effects of changes in U_2 are in general ambiguous in their signs. To overcome this difficulty and also to characterise the economy's dynamics, we use numerical analysis. In Appendix 2 we discuss the assumed values of the exogenous parameters of the model. We also report the values taken by the model's endogenous variables, while here we make use of their graphs.

An unanticipated increase in U_1. Consider first the impact effects of an unanticipated increase in the demand for real bonds:

$$\frac{dP_{K(o)}}{dU_1} = \frac{-1_3}{1_1} \; \frac{d\overline{B}}{dU_1} \; < 0$$

$$\frac{dS_{(o)}}{dU_1} = \theta'_2 \frac{dP_{K(o)}}{dU_1} > 0$$

and

$$\frac{dQ_{(o)}}{dU_1} = Q_S \frac{dS_{(o)}}{dU_1} < 0$$

As we have seen earlier, an increase in U_1 will increase the long-run stock of real bonds. However, long-run changes in the stock of real bonds can occur only through current account imbalances and hence through short-run changes in the real exchange rate. Therefore, an increase in the long-run stock of real bonds can only be achieved through a short-run rise in S.

We can now describe how a U_1 shock affects the economy in the short run and over time by making use of Figures 3.12(a)–(e).

An unanticipated increase in U_1 will increase the short-run demand for real bonds. Since, in the short run the stock of real bonds is predetermined, the market price of capital, P_K, will have to fall to reduce real wealth and thus maintain equilibrium in the market for real bonds (see Figure 3.12(a)). Given the definition of ρ, the fall in P_K will lead to an increase in the real domestic interest rate. It will also reduce domestic investment, thus creating an excess supply in the domestic output market. Since in the short run the stock of capital is predetermined, the real exchange rate will have to depreciate to maintain equilibrium in the output market, (see Figures 3.12(b–d)).

Over time, however, the stock of capital and the stock of real bonds will change: the short-run fall in P_K, by inducing short-run disinvestment, will lead to an initial fall in the stock of capital (see Figures 3.12(b–e)). On the other hand, the short-run real exchange rate depreciation, by creating a current account surplus, will increase the stock of real bonds (see Figure 3.12(e)). The initial fall in the capital stock and the increase in the stock of real bonds will jointly create an excess supply in the market for real bonds and thus an increase in P_K will be required to maintain equilibrium in the real bond market. Moreover, the increase in P_K and the initial fall in the capital stock will create an excess demand for domestic output. Thus the real exchange rate will have to appreciate to maintain equilibrium in the goods market. As a result, over time, P_K will increase and S will fall until they return to their initial steady-state values (see graph 12(b)). After its initial fall, the capital stock will also increase since the rise in P_K (the profitability of capital) will induce capital formation. Thus K will return eventually to its initial steady-state level (see Figures 3.12(b–e)).

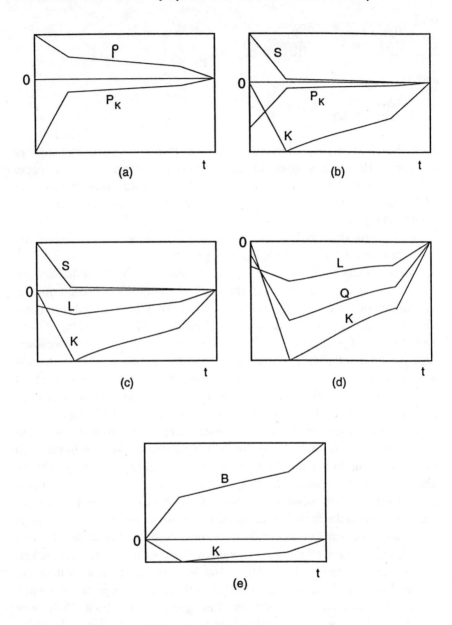

Figure 3.12 Paths of adjustment of real interest rate; price of capital; real exchange rate; capital stock; employment level; domestic output and the stock of real bonds under an unanticipated increase in the demand for real bonds

We now turn our analysis to the dynamic adjustment of domestic employment and domestic output, illustrated in Figures 3.12(c, d). As the real exchange rate appreciates over time, domestic employment tends to increase. At the same time, the initial fall in K tends to reduce domestic output. However, as both domestic employment and the capital stock are increasing, domestic output will increase over time returning to its initial steady-state level.

An unanticipated increase in U_2. Let us now consider the impact effects of an aggregate demand shock. We first consider the impact effect of an increase in U_2 on the market price of capital, P_K. From equation (26) we obtain the expression:

$$\frac{dP_{K(o)}}{dU_1} = (2\delta - \frac{l_2}{l_1})\ \frac{d\overline{K}}{dU_2} - \frac{l_3}{l_1}\ \frac{d\overline{B}}{dU_2} \gtreqless 0$$

Two opposing forces are in operation here making the sign of this expression ambiguous. The first is the effect of a fall in the long-run capital stock on the short-run value of P_K. This effect is negative. The second is the effect of a fall in the long-run stock of real bonds on P_K and is positive. As far as the first effect is concerned, this results from the fact that a fall in the long-run stock of capital requires short-run disinvestment and thus a low profitability of capital, i.e. a low P_K. As for the second effect, this arises from the fact that a fall in the long-run stock of real bonds requires a short-run current account deficit, which in turn requires a short-run appreciation of the real exchange rate. This fall in S, however, can be achieved through a higher P_K, (which, by increasing domestic investment and thus the demand for domestic output, will result in a fall in S). Therefore, overall, the sign of the impact effect of a U_2 shock on P_K is unclear. To overcome this ambiguity we resort to numerical analysis (see Appendix 2). This indicates that the impact effect of an increase in U_2 on P_K is negative and relatively small.

We turn now to the impact effect of an increase in U_2 on real exchange rate and domestic output:

$$\frac{dS_{(o)}}{dU_2} = \theta'_2\ \frac{dP_{K(o)}}{dU_2} + \frac{1}{\theta_1} < 0$$

and

$$\frac{dQ_{(o)}}{dU_2} = Q_S \ \frac{dS}{dU_2} > 0$$

We shall describe the short-run and dynamic effects of the shock by making use of Figures 3.13(a–d). An unanticipated increase in U_2 will create an excess demand for domestic output. Equilibrium in the market for domestic output will require a fall in both S and P_K. The fall in S will increase domestic employment and thus domestic production (Figure 3.13(e)). The fall in S will also reduce net exports and aggregate demand. On the other hand, the fall in P_K, by reducing investment, will leave more units of output available to meet the higher consumption demand for domestic output (created by the increase in U_2). As a result of these effects the excess demand for domestic output will be eliminated. At the same time, given the definition of ρ, the fall in P_K will increase the real interest rate and this will in turn reduce the demand for real bonds. Hence, P_K will have to increase to maintain equilibrium in the market for real bonds. However, our numerical analysis suggests that on balance P_K will fall in the short run. This is shown in Figure 3.13(a), where both P_K and S are lower than their initial steady-state values.

Over time, the stock of real bonds and the stock of capital will change: the short-run real exchange rate appreciation, by creating a current account deficit, will lead over time to a fall in the stock of real bonds, (Figure 3.13(d)). By creating excess demand for real bonds, it will require a fall in P_K, to maintain equilibrium in the asset market. The fall in P_K, by reducing the profitability of capital, will lead in the short run and over time to a gradual decline in the capital stock (Figure 3.13(c–d)). Furthermore, the fall over time in P_K, by reducing investment, will create an excess supply of domestic output, thus requiring a rise in S over time to keep the goods market in equilibrium (see Figure 3.13(a)).

Figure 3.13(c) illustrates the dynamic adjustment of domestic employment and domestic output. Domestic employment and output fall over time due to the fall in the stock of capital and the depreciation of the real exchange rate.

The Role of International Labour Mobility in the Short Run and the Dynamic Adjustment of the Economy to Unanticipated U shocks

As noted earlier, because the real exchange rate remains unchanged from one steady-state to the other, the presence of ILM does not affect the long-run properties of the model. However, because in the short run and over time the

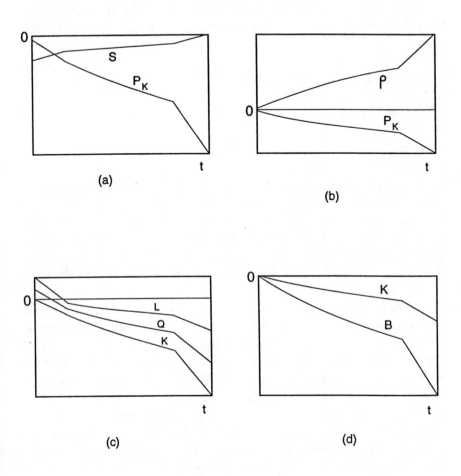

(a)

(b)

(c)

(d)

Figure 3.13 Paths of adjustment of real interest rate; price of capital; real exchange rate; capital stock; employment level; domestic output and the stock of real bonds under an unanticipated increase in the demand for domestic output

real exchange rate changes, it may affect the impact and the dynamic effects of the unanticipated shocks U_1 and U_2.

To investigate whether or not the presence of ILM will affect the short run and dynamic adjustment of the economy to the shocks, we consider three cases:

'Low ILM': $C_1 = 1$ and $C_2 = 0.2$

'Moderate ILM': $C_1 = 1$ and $C_2 = 0.5$

'High ILM': $C_1 = 1$ and $C_2 = 1$

Our numerical results, reported in Appendix 2, suggest that the degree of ILM affects both the impact effects and the time paths of L, Q and S, as can be seen from Figures 3.14 (a–c) and 3.15 (a–c). Indeed, we can distinguish here three effects of ILM: (a) the employment effect; (b) the output effect; and (c) the real exchange rate effect. Through these three effects, the presence of ILM is shown to affect the accumulation of capital as well as the accumulation of real bonds.

We shall analyse these effects for each shock. Consider first the impact effects of the change in U_1. As we have seen earlier, an unanticipated increase in U_1 causes a real exchange rate depreciation in the short run. This induces workers to undertake more work abroad, resulting in a fall in domestic employment. The higher the degree of ILM the stronger the response of the domestic workforce to the real exchange rate depreciation and thus the greater the fall in domestic employment. The 'employment effect' is illustrated in Figure 3.14(a), where L_1, L_2 and L_3 correspond to the case of low, moderate and high ILM respectively. In the first two cases of ILM, the short run fall in domestic employment (L_1, L_2) is less than its fall over time (caused by the initial fall in the capital stock). With high ILM, the short-run fall in domestic employment exceeds its fall over time. In fact, having fallen to its lower point in the short run, domestic employment increases over time before returning to its initial steady-state value.

The 'employment effect' in turn creates an 'output effect': increased ILM leads to a larger fall in output both in the short-run and over time (see Figure 3.14(b)).

The 'output effect' in turn creates a 'real exchange rate effect'. This effect works through the goods market equilibrium condition: because increased ILM is associated with a larger fall in output, a smaller rise in S is required to

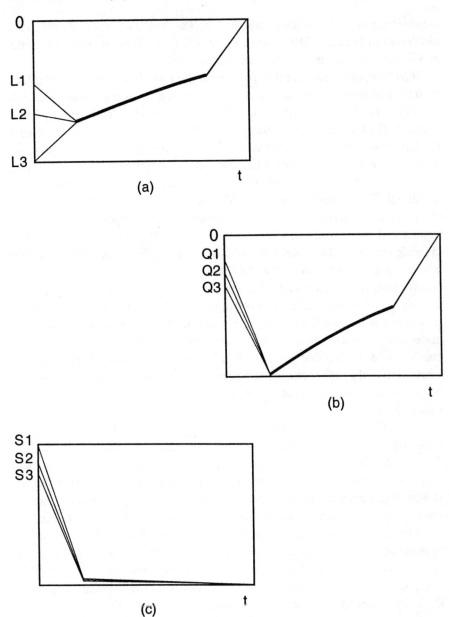

**Figure 3.14 Paths of adjustment of real exchange rate; employment
level and domestic output in the case of an unanticipated
increase in the demand for real bonds and under different
degrees of ILM: low; moderate and high ILM**

maintain equilibrium in the goods market. The 'real exchange rate effect' is illustrated in Figure 3.14(c): as the value of C_2 increases, the size of the rise in S in the short run and its fall over time decreases.

The 'output effect' and the 'real exchange rate effect' will in turn affect both the accumulation of capital and the accumulation of real bonds. We shall examine first the accumulation of real bonds. Due to the 'real exchange rate effect' of ILM the accumulation of real bonds will be lower. Indeed, increased ILM, by resulting a lower real exchange rate depreciation both on impact and over time, will lead to a lower current account surplus and thus to a lower accumulation rate of real bonds over time. Consider, next, the accumulation of capital. The 'output effect' of ILM will result a larger fall in the capital stock. Indeed, increased ILM, by resulting a lower output supply both on impact and over time, will require a larger fall in P_K to keep equilibrium in the goods market. Thus, increased ILM, by lowering the profitability of capital will result a larger fall in the capital stock.

We turn now to the impact effects of an aggregate demand shock. An unanticipated increase in U_2, by creating excess demand for domestic output, will cause a real exchange rate appreciation. This will induce workers to undertake more work in the home country thus resulting in a rise in domestic employment. As the degree of ILM increases the response of the domestic workforce to the real exchange rate appreciation also increases resulting in a larger rise in domestic employment. This 'employment effect' is illustrated in Figure 3.15(a).

Over time, as the real exchange rate depreciates and the capital stock falls, employment is reduced. The 'output effect' of ILM is illustrated in Figure 3.15(b), that is, the higher the degree of ILM the larger the rise in domestic output in the short-run and the larger the fall over time. The 'output effect' of ILM reduces the magnitude of the short-run real exchange rate appreciation: see Figure 3.15(c), where an increase in C_2 lowers the size of the fall in S.

The 'output effect' and the 'real exchange rate effect' will in turn affect both the accumulation of capital and the accumulation of real bonds. Consider, first, the accumulation of real bonds. The 'real exchange rate effect' of ILM will reduce the rate of decrease in the stock of real bonds. Indeed, increased ILM, by resulting a lower real exchange rate appreciation will lead to a relatively lower current account deficit and thus to a lower decrease in the stock of real bonds over time. Consider, next, the accumulation of capital. The 'output effect' of ILM will result a lower fall in the capital stock. Indeed, increased ILM, by resulting a higher output supply both on impact and over

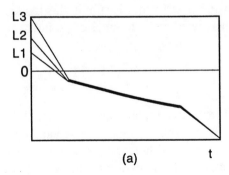

(a)

t

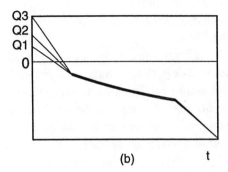

(b)

t

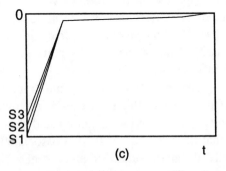

(c)

t

Figure 3.15 Paths of adjustment of real exchange rate; employment level and domestic output in the case of an unanticipated increase in the demand for domestic output and under different degrees of ILM: low; moderate and high ILM

time, will require a lower fall in P_K to keep equilibrium in this market. The lower fall in P_K will in turn result a lower fall in the stock of capital over time.

6   Conclusions

The model analysed in chapter 1 bears the limitation that the capital stock of the economy is taken to be fixed. In this chapter we have extended our model of ILM to allow for changes over time in the capital stock. We have also extended our analysis in that chapter by considering the effects of two unanticipated non-monetary shocks namely, unanticipated exogenous increases in the demand for real bonds and for domestic goods.

An unanticipated increase in the demand for real bonds leads to results similar to those obtained in the case of the monetary expansion analysed in chapter 1.

As far as the effects of the aggregate demand shock are concerned, these are in line with the literature on capital formation. Like, for example, Tobin and Buiter (1976), Pikoulakis (1984) and Murphy (1989), we find that an unanticipated increase in the demand for domestic output will on impact cause a real exchange rate appreciation and that, by 'crowding-out' investment, will lead to a reduction in the steady-state stock of capital.

The main difference between our model and the existing literature on capital accumulation lies in our assumption about labour supply. Most of the literature on capital formation assumes that labour is supplied inelastically, while in our model we adopt the more general assumption that labour supply depends on both the real domestic wage and the real foreign wage in terms of domestic-currency purchasing power units, through international labour mobility. Therefore, changes in the real exchange rate will affect the economy in our model through two channels: by changing the domestic real consumption wage; and by generating labour inflows and outflows.

Although the presence of ILM does not affect the long-run properties of the model, it affects the size of the impact effects, as well as the dynamic adjustment of the economy in response to the two unanticipated shocks. In particular, our analysis shows that the presence of ILM is associated with three effects: 'an employment effect', 'an output effect' and 'a real exchange rate effect'. That is, the presence of ILM, by increasing the sensitivity of labour supply to changes in the real exchange rate, will increase the sensitivity of domestic employment and domestic output to changes in the real exchange rate, induced by the two unanticipated shocks. In the context of our model, where capital is not mobile internationally, our findings suggest that the presence of ILM reduces the variability of the real exchange rate following each shock. Finally, the presence of ILM affects, through the above effects, both the accumulation of capital and the accumulation of real bonds.

Notes

1   See also Gould (1968) and Pikoulakis (1981).
2   As we show in Appendix 2 the GG-locus is strictly concave to the origin.
3   i.e.

$$\frac{dQ}{dU_i} = Q_S \frac{dS}{dU_i} \tag{21}$$

4   In deriving the stable path we have followed the methodology explained in Eaton and Turnovsky (1983) and Zervoyianni (1988).

5    $\sigma_o = \mu_o \psi_2 C_1 S^{(\psi_2 C_3)} K^{(\psi_2 C_1 - 1)} > 0$

Appendix 1

Using bars to denote initial steady-state values and differentiating equations (14), (15) and (16), we obtain:

$$d\rho = - b'_2 \, dP_K - b'_1 \, dU_1 \tag{a}$$

$$d\rho = \frac{Q_{KS}}{\overline{P}_K} \, dS - \frac{Q_K}{(\overline{P}_K)^2} \, dP_K \tag{b}$$

$$-\theta_2 \, dP_K + \theta_1 \, dS = dU_2 \tag{c}$$

where

$$b'_1 = \frac{1}{F_1 \overline{w}} \quad < 0$$

$$b'_2 = \frac{\overline{F}(..)}{F_1 \overline{w}} \quad < 0$$

$$\theta_1 = (1 - D') \, Q_S - X'(.) < 0$$

$$\theta_2 = I'(.) > 0$$

From equations (α)–(c) the impact effects of the two shocks are:

U₁ shock

$$\frac{dP_K}{dU_1} = \frac{1}{\overline{w} F_1 V_3} \quad < 0$$

$$\frac{dS}{dU_1} = \frac{\theta'_2}{\overline{w} F_1 V_3} \quad > 0$$

$$\frac{d\rho}{dU_1} = \frac{\varphi_1 \theta'_2 - \varphi_3}{\overline{w} F_1 V_3} > 0$$

U_2 shock

$$\frac{dP_K}{dU_2} = \frac{Z_4}{\theta_1 V_3} > 0$$

$$\frac{dS}{dU_2} = \frac{Z_2}{\theta_1 V_3} < 0$$

$$\frac{d\rho}{dU_2} = \frac{\varphi_1 Z_2 - \varphi_3 Z_4}{\theta_1 V_3} > 0$$

where

$$Z_2 = \varphi_3 - b'_2 = \frac{Q_K}{(\overline{P_K})^2} - \frac{F(..)}{F_1 \overline{w}} > 0$$

$$Z_4 = \frac{\varphi_1}{\overline{P_K}} = \frac{Q_{KS}}{\overline{P_K}} < 0$$

$$\theta'_2 = \frac{I'(.)}{(1-D') Q_S - X'(.)} < 0$$

$$V_3 = Z_2 - Z_4 \theta'_2 > 0$$

Slopes of the $\rho\rho$ and BB loci

$$\frac{dP_K}{dS}\bigg|_{\rho\rho \text{ locus}} = \frac{\overline{P_K} \varphi_1}{\varphi_3} = \frac{\overline{P_K} Q_{KS}}{Q_K} < 0$$

$$\frac{dP_K}{dS}\bigg|_{BB \text{ locus}} = \frac{\theta_1}{\theta_2} < 0$$

The GG locus is assumed to be steeper than the $\rho\rho$ locus. This is guaranteed by the condition $Q_{KS}\,\theta'_2 - Q_K < 0$

Convexity of $\rho\rho$ locus

From the reduced-form equation for Q in section 1 we obtain

$$\frac{d^2P_K}{dS^2} \;=\; \frac{\alpha c_3 \psi_1 \overline{P}_K}{S^2} \;>\; 0$$

Concavity of the GG locus

$$\frac{d^2P_K}{dS^2} \;=\; \frac{1}{I'(.)}\left[\,(1\text{-}D')\,Q_{ss} - \frac{1}{2}\left(\frac{\theta_1}{\theta_2}\right)^2\,\right]\;<\;0$$

since

$$I''(P_K) = h'(P_K) = \frac{1}{2} = G'_{P_K}$$

Appendix 2

For the numerical analysis we have assumed the following parameter values, which are similar to most existing papers using numerical analysis, see e.g. Bhandari and Genberg (1989) and Zervoyianni (1992).

Non ILM Parameters

$\alpha = 0.5, \bar{B} = 0.3733, \bar{K} = 1, \bar{S} = 1, \delta = 0.06, \bar{F}(..) = 0.25, c_1 = 1, \bar{w} = 1.49,$

$I'(.) = \dfrac{H'(.)}{H''(.)} = \dfrac{\bar{P}_K}{2} = 0.56, F_1 = -5, \bar{U}_1 = 1, \bar{U}_2 = 0.09, X'(.) = 0.5, D_2 = 0.9$

Numerical values for the paths of the endogenous variables are reported below, where for any reported variable X_{ij} the first subscript indicates the unanticipated shock, i.e. $(1) = U_1$ or $(2) = U_2$, while the second one indicates the case of international mobility, i.e. $(1) =$ low, $(2) =$ moderate, $(3) =$ high.

Time	K_{11}	K_{12}	K_{13}	B_{11}	B_{12}
0	0.00	0.00	0.00	0.00	0.00
1	-.31323	-.31469	-.31509	.56513	.56147
2	-.25726	-.25780	-.25805	.70240	.69846
3	-.21129	-.21200	-.21357	.81514	.81113
4	-.17354	-.17411	-.17557	.90774	.90381
5	0.00	0.00	0.00	1.3333	1.3333

Time	P_{K11}	P_{K12}	P_{K13}	S_{11}	S_{12}
0	-.20607	-.20626	-.20657	.22555	.22333
1	-.035120	-.035304	-.035603	.0060490	.0060320
2	-.028846	-.029038	-.029355	.0049680	.0049620
3	-.023691	-.023885	-.024204	.0040800	.0040810
4	-.019458	-.019646	-.019957	.0027520	.0033570
5	0.00	0.00	0.00	0.00	0.00

Time	Q_{11}	Q_{12}	Q_{13}	L_{11}	L_{12}
0	-.033081	-.048380	-.073240	-.066161	-.096770
1	-.20980	-.21110	-.21235	-.10619	-.10701
2	-.17284	-.17344	-.17395	-.089111	-.089430
3	-.14235	-.14288	-.14421	-.072124	-.072737
4	-.11681	-.11748	-.11861	-.058828	-.059828
5	0.00	0.00	0.00	0.00	0.00

Time	ρ_{11}	ρ_{12}	ρ_{13}	K_{21}	K_{22}
0	.12703	.12703	.12702	0.00	0.00
1	.064243	.064549	.065052	-1.0784	-1.0709
2	.052763	.053093	.053636	-2.0111	-1.9986
3	.043335	.043671	.044004	-2.7772	-2.7616
4	.035591	.035920	.03610	-3.4063	-3.3893
5	0.00	0.00	0.00	-6.2981	-6.2981

Time	B_{21}	B_{22}	B_{23}	P_{K21}	P_{K22}
0	0.00	0.00	0.00	-.018674	-.018508
1	-2.8449	-2.8252	-2.7929	-.17051	-.16936
2	-5.1323	-5.1006	-5.0484	-.27509	-.27343
3	-7.0110	-6.9721	-6.9081	-.36098	-.35903
4	-8.5540	-8.5116	-8.4415	-.43153	-.42945
5	-15.9760	-15.9760	-15.9760	-.75577	-.75577

Time	S_{21}	S_{22}	S_{23}	Q_{21}	Q_{22}
0	-.15547	-.15398	-.15116	.022802	.033362
1	-.10080	-.10020	-.099205	-.70416	-.69222
2	-.082788	-.082414	-.081796	-1.3286	-1.3145
3	-.067995	-.067788	-.067443	-1.8415	-1.8264
4	-.055845	-.055757	-.055608	-2.2627	-2.2474
5	0.00	0.00	0.00	-4.1987	-4.1987

Time	L_{21}	L_{22}	L_{23}	ρ_{21}	ρ_{22}
0	.045603	.066724	.10104	-.6250E-3	-.6200E-3
1	-.32990	-.31355	-.28672	.23961	.23795
2	-.64609	-.63048	-.60481	.43091	.42824
3	-.90577	-.89117	-.86708	.58802	.58476
4	-1.1191	-1.1056	-1.0833	.71705	.71350
5	-2.0994	-2.0994	-2.0994	1.3101	1.3101

Time	B_{13}	S_{13}	L_{13}	K_{23}	P_{K23}
0	0.00	.21973	-.14649	0.00	-.018237
1	.55547	.0060040	-.10770	-1.0586	-.16747
2	.69197	.0049500	-.090044	-1.9780	-.27071
3	.80452	.0040820	-.073358	-2.7361	-.35803
4	.89732	.0039650	-.060128	-3.3612	-.42801
5	1.3330	0.00	0.00	-6.2981	-.75577

Time	Q_{23}	ρ_{23}
0	.050519	-.6110E-3
1	-.67265	.23524
2	-1.2914	.42387
3	-1.8016	.57939
4	-2.2223	.70763
5	-4.1987	1.3101

4   Trade Union Behaviour and International Migration of Labour

1   Introduction

In the previous chapters we have considered the macroeconomic effects of international migration of labour (IML) under the assumption of competitive labour markets. The labour markets of most countries, however, do not conform with this assumption: many western countries are currently experiencing a persistently high level of unemployment; and changes in the marginal revenue product of labour are usually accompanied by changes in the level of employment rather than in real wages. These two stylised facts of today's economies, unemployment and real wage rigidity, should in principle be taken into account in examining the macroeconomic implications of international migration of labour. Yet, as Brecher and Choudhri (1987) note, much of the theoretical literature on IML assumes full employment. Few exceptions are the papers by Bhagwati and Hamada (1974, 1975), McCulloch and Yellen (1975), Rodriguez (1975) and Djajic (1985). These papers, however, assume a non market-clearing wage that is set administratively (by, for example, minimum wage legislation).

Contemporary economic theory suggests three approaches to unemployment and rigid wages that differ from the traditional consideration of minimum wage legislation. The first is the 'implicit contracts' theory which assumes that firms supply their workers with insurance against income uncertainty. This results in a relatively stable real wage. The second is the 'trade union' model which is based on the assumption that trade unions have some bargaining power over wages and/or employment. The third approach is the 'efficiency wages' theory which assumes that labour effort is related to real wages offered by firms. To date, no attempt has been made in the literature to incorporate the possibility of IML into these three models of unemployment.

110

The aim of this chapter is to incorporate the possibility of IML into a trade union model of a small open economy with a flexible exchange rate. Our motivation comes from Brecher and Choudhri (1987) who argue that IML will cause a partial adjustment in the wage rate even if this wage rate is set unilaterally by a trade union or by a firm through efficiency wage considerations.

Our choice in this chapter of a trade union approach rather than an efficiency wage approach is based on two considerations. First, as Nickell (1990) notes, 'we have some evidence in favour of the efficiency wage story but it is not, as yet, overwhelming'. Second, trade unions play a decisive role in wage-employment decisions in many industrial countries, particularly in Europe (see, e.g. Layard, Nickell and Jackman, (1991,1994) and Lindbeck (1993)).

We will restrict our analysis to the case of a small open economy which faces outflows of labour (emigration). We will also assume that the economy is made up of many identical firms, all unionised. This assumption allows us to consider the wage-employment bargaining within an individual firm as a microcosm of the entire labour market wage-employment bargaining. Throughout the chapter we shall further assume that the union is concerned only with the welfare of its existing members and wishes to maximise the expected utility of its median member.

In section 2 that follows we present the efficient bargains model of trade unions in the closed-economy case. In this model the union and the firm bargain over the joint determination of the wage rate and the level of employment. The outcome of this bargaining is Pareto efficient, i.e. it lies on the contract curve.

In section 3 we extend the efficient bargains model to the open-economy case, and in section 4 we open up the economy to international migration. The decision to migrate or not is assumed to be based on the existing wage differential between the small open economy and the rest of the world. In this context, migration outflows reduce the membership of the trade union. Since the union is concerned with the welfare of its existing members, lower membership results in higher wages as there are fewer union jobs to be protected. Hence employment and union membership remain lower after the migration flows have ceased and unemployment may be lower or unchanged depending on whether or not 'outsiders' are migrating.

We also find that, through international migration, the home real consumer wage is positively related to the rest-of-the-world wage and negatively related to average migration cost: an increase in the rest-of-the-world wage or a decrease in the migration cost induces a larger proportion of insiders to migrate abroad. Therefore, the smaller number of remaining insiders, acting through their union, will succeed in achieving higher real consumer wages at home. On the other hand, an increase in the real exchange rate increases the home real product wage. However, the sign of change in the home real consumer wage is ambiguous. Finally, a positive technological shock by strengthening the bargaining position of the trade union, leads to an increase in both the real consumer wage and the employment level. Section 5 contains concluding comments.

2   The Efficient Bargains Model of Trade Unions in the Closed-Economy Case

We consider an economy that is made up of many identical firms, all unionised. Thus, the wage-employment activity within an individual firm may be seen as a microcosm of the wage-employment activity of the entire labour market.

Trade unions theory is based on the idea that unions are concerned only with the welfare of their existing members and aim to maximise an objective function. The specification, however, of the union's objective may take a variety of functional forms. Following Layard, Nickell and Jackman (1991) we shall assume here that the union wishes to maximise the expected utility of its median voter. We may, then, specify the union's objective function as

$$V = [U(\omega) - U(\chi)] \quad \min\left(\frac{L}{L_0}, 1\right) \tag{1}$$

where

$\omega \equiv \dfrac{W}{P}$ is the real product wage

$\chi \equiv \dfrac{X}{P}$ is the real layoff pay; which is the income equivalen of not being employed

W is the money wage
X is the money layoff pay
P is the GDP deflator
L_0 is the initial membership of the union (taken to be exogenous)

L is employment

$U(\omega)$ is the utility of the median voter derived from the real wage, net of the disutility of work

$U(\chi)$ is the utility derived from not working

$\dfrac{L}{L_0}$ is the probability of the median voter to be employed for $L \leq L_0$.

Equation (1) is based on the assumption that the union maximises the expected utility of its median member

$$V = \frac{L}{L_0} U(\omega) + (1 - \frac{L}{L_0}) U(\chi) \qquad (1a)$$

where

$$\frac{L}{L_0} \text{ and } (1 - \frac{L}{L_0})$$

is the probability that the median voter will be employed and unemployed, respectively. Further simplification allows us to write

$$V = \frac{L}{L_0} [U(\omega) - U(\chi)] + U(\chi) \qquad \text{if } L \leq L_0 \qquad (1b)$$

and

$$V = U(\omega) \qquad \text{if } L > L_0 \qquad (1c)$$

The first expression for $V(.)$, corresponds to the case where the median member has no secure employment, while the second one, (1c), corresponds to the case of secure employment (see Oswald, (1986), Carruth and Oswald, (1987) and Creedy and MacDonald (1991) for a detailed analysis). Throughout this chapter we focus on the case of a non-secured employment for the median voter and hence we use the first expression for $V(.)$. Here we adopt a functional form for $V(.)$, equation (1), proposed by Layard, Nickell and Jackman (1991) which is equivalent to (1b) since $U(\chi)$ is a constant.

With the union's objective function given by (1) the pattern of the indifference curves is depicted in Figure 4.1. That is, the indifference curves in the (ω, L) space are 'kinked'. They are rectangular hyperbolas, asymptotic to $\omega = \chi$ for $L \leq L_0$, while for $L > L_0$ they are horizontal. In other words, when employment is less than the union membership, the union is prepared to trade wages for employment. On the other hand, when employment exceeds the union membership, the union places no value on further employment since the median member is always employed and he is then only concerned with his wage.

Formally, the slope of an indifference curve is given by

$$\frac{d\omega}{dL} = - \frac{\omega}{L\epsilon} \tag{2}$$

where ϵ is the elasticity of the excess utility from work with respect to the wage, and is defined as

$$\epsilon \equiv \frac{\omega U'(\omega)}{U(\omega) - U(\chi)} \tag{3}$$

Next we turn our analysis to the firm's objective. We formalise the firm's objective in a conventional way: we assume that the firm wants to maximise real profits. Let $f(L)$ be a strictly concave production function. Then, real profits π are given by

$$\pi = f(L) - \omega L \tag{4}$$

Partially differentiating the real profit function with respect to L and setting the result (π_L) equal to zero, we obtain the familiar downward sloping labour demand curve:

$$f'(L) = \omega \tag{5}$$

With the objective function of the firm given by (4) the family of isoprofit curves in the (ω, L) space is depicted in Figure 4.2. Each isoprofit curve is concave from below. The locus of the maximum points of the isoprofit curves is the labour demand curve, since the labour demand curve defines the profit-maximising employment at any wage. Hence, isoprofit curves are upward sloping to the left of the labour demand curve and downward sloping to the right of the labour demand schedule. Formally, the slope of an isoprofit curve is given by

$$\frac{d\omega}{dL} = \frac{f'(L) - \omega}{L} \tag{6}$$

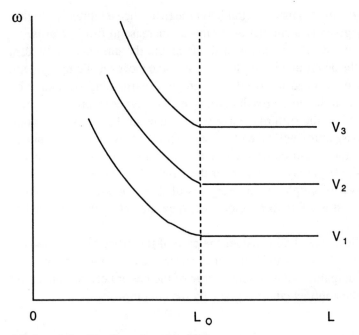

Figure 4.1   Trade unions' indifference curves
(by permission of the *Economic Record* (1991), Vol. 61, p. 348.)

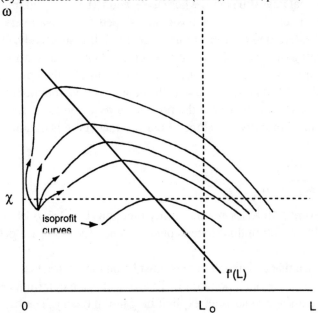

Figure 4.2   Firms' isoprofit curves

A lower isoprofit curve is more desirable for the firm since it represents higher profits: for any given L, a smaller ω implies an increase in firm's profits.

Having analysed the objectives of the firm and the union, we now turn our analysis to the determination of the wage rate and the level of employment. For this purpose we need to specify the process (bargaining structure) by which the firm and the union reach agreement. Two types of processes may be considered. First, the firm may have complete control over employment, in which case bargaining will take place only over the wage rate. Bargains of this type are on the labour demand curve and are Pareto inefficient. Second, the union and the firm may bargain over the joint determination of the wage rate and the level of employment. Bargains of this type are off the labour demand curve and are Pareto efficient, i.e. they are 'efficient bargains' or 'efficient contracts'.

In what follows we shall consider the case of the efficient bargains, i.e. points of tangency between an indifference curve and an isoprofit curve. The set of efficient bargains is the contract curve of the barter between the union and the firm. The contract curve is given by the condition

$$\epsilon = \frac{\omega}{\omega - f'(L)} \tag{7}$$

It starts from the real payoff pay (χ), where $\omega = \chi$ and $f'(L) = \chi$, and may be vertical for a risk-neutral worker or positively sloped for a risk-averse worker. The two cases are depicted in Figures 4.3 and 4.4, respectively. In what follows we shall assume a risk-averse worker and hence our analysis will be based on Figure 4.4, where the contract curve is shown by the upward sloping curve from A to B. At A, where $\omega = \chi$, the contract curve touches the labour demand curve $f'(L)$. At B, where the profits are assumed to be zero, the contract curve ends. Formally, the slope of the contract curve is obtained by differentiating (7):

$$\frac{d\omega}{dL} = \frac{U'(\omega) \, f''(L)}{U''(\omega) \, [\omega - f'(L)]} \tag{8}$$

This slope goes to infinity for a risk-neutral utility function ($U''(.) = 0$) while for a risk-averse utility function this slope is positive since for $\omega > \chi$ we get $\omega > f'(L)$.

While we have seen that efficient bargains must lie on the contract curve, we are not still able to single out a point on it. To arrive at some determinate point on the contract curve, we need an explicit bargaining theory. The best known formal solution to the bargaining problem is the Nash bargaining

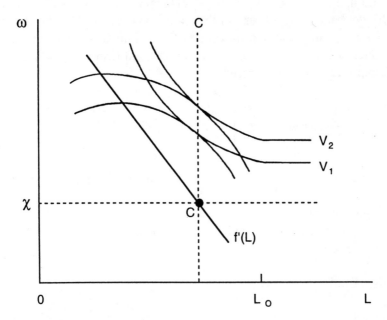

Figure 4.3 Efficient bargains and the contract curve in the case of a risk-neutral worker

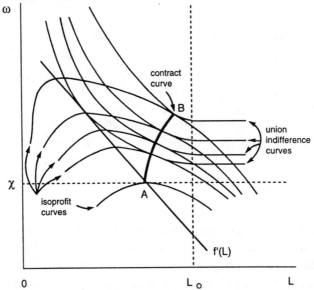

Figure 4.4 Efficient bargains and the contract curve in the case of a risk-averse worker

solution. Following Creedy and McDonald (1991) we will assume here different bargaining powers for the union and the firm. Thus the asymmetric Nash bargaining solution maximises the weighted geometric mean (Nash product or Nash maximand) of the union's and firm's pay-offs. Hence, the Nash product to be maximised is

$$N = \left\{ \frac{L}{L_0} \, U(\omega) - U(\chi) \right\}^{\frac{\Phi}{1+\Phi}} \, [f(L) - \omega L]^{\frac{1}{1+\Phi}} \tag{9}$$

where the weights $\frac{\Phi}{1+\Phi}$ and $\frac{1}{1+\Phi}$ are the bargaining powers of the union and the firm respectively.

Differentiation of (9) with respect to ω and with respect to L gives the first order conditions:

$$\epsilon = \frac{\omega}{\omega - f'(L)} \tag{10}$$

$$\omega = \frac{1}{1+\Phi} \left[\frac{\Phi f(L)}{L} + f'(L) \right] \tag{11}$$

Equation (10), as we have seen earlier, defines the contract curve of efficient bargains. This result is not surprising since the derivation of Nash solution uses Pareto optimality as one of its axioms. The new element, owed to the Nash bargaining solution, is equation (11) which we may call the 'power locus' (PL). McDonald and Solow (1981) call it the 'equity locus', as they assume equal bargaining powers for the firm and the union, i.e.$\Phi = 1$. With $\Phi \neq 1$, PL is a weighted average of the average and marginal product of labour, with weights equal to

$$\frac{\Phi}{1+\Phi} \quad \text{and} \quad \frac{1}{1+\Phi}$$

respectively. Given the concavity of the production function, both the average and the marginal product of labour are decreasing. As a result, PL is negatively sloped as illustrated in Figure 4.5. The PL starts from point C, which lies on the isoprofit curve of zero profits and on the labour demand curve, since at point C we have that

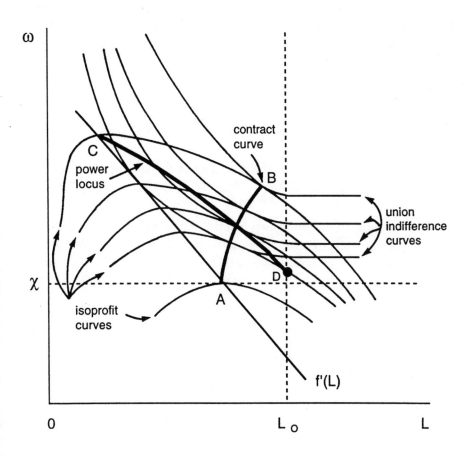

**Figure 4.5   Efficient bargains and the joint determination of real wage
and employment level**
(by permission of the *Economic Record* (1991), Vol. 61, p. 351.)

$$\omega = f'(L) = \frac{f(L)}{L} \qquad (12)$$

whatever the value of Φ. Moreover, the power locus ends at point D where $L = L_0$, since we have assumed that the union is concerned with the welfare of its existing members. An algebraic expression for the slope of PL can be obtained by differentiating (11):

$$\frac{d\omega}{dL} = \frac{\Phi}{1+\Phi} \left[\frac{(\alpha - 1)f(.)}{L^2} + \frac{f''(.)}{\Phi} \right] < 0$$

where

$$\alpha \equiv \frac{Lf'(.)}{f(.)} \quad \text{is the elasticity of the production function with respect to employment.}$$

The concavity of the production function requires $f'' < 0$ and $\alpha < 1$. Hence the slope of PL is negative. Moreover, an increase in the value of Φ will shift the power locus to the right. To show this, assume a powerful union which forces the firm to operate along its zero-isoprofit curve, i.e. $\Phi \to \infty$. In this case the power locus is

$$\omega = \frac{f(.)}{L}$$

That is, the real product wage is equal to the average product of labour ($\pi = 0$). On the other hand, a powerless union, i.e. $\Phi = 0$, will accept a real product wage and employment level on the labour demand curve. The power locus in this case coincides with the labour demand curve:

$$\omega = f'(L)$$

The intersection of the upward sloping contract curve and the downward sloping power locus determines the bargained wage. Substituting (11) into (10) one can obtain an algebraic expression for the bargained wage

$$\epsilon = \frac{\Phi + \alpha}{\Phi(1-\alpha)} \qquad (13)$$

where ϵ, as we have seen earlier, is a function of ω and χ.

Equation (13) states that the bargained wage is a mark-up on the layoff pay χ, in terms of utility.

A well known result of trade union models is that shifts in the labour demand curve, resulting from technological shocks, will not affect the bargained wage if α, Φ and layoff pay χ remain unchanged. On the contrary, output fluctuations will fall entirely on employment. To show this, we follow Blanchard and Fischer (1989) in assuming that the firm's real profits are given by

$$\pi = \theta f(L) - \omega L \tag{14}$$

where θ is a technological shock. The first-order conditions are now given by

$$\epsilon = \frac{\omega}{\omega - \theta f'(L)} \quad \text{(contract curve)} \tag{15}$$

and

$$\omega = \frac{1}{1+\Phi} \left[\frac{\Phi \theta f(L)}{L} + \theta f'(L) \right] \quad \text{(power locus)} \tag{16}$$

While the contract curve and the power locus are now given by (15) and (16), equation (13), which determines the bargained wage, remains unchanged. This is because Φ is exogenous and the elasticity of production function, α, is independent of the shock. Therefore, shifts in labour demand will not change the real wage. With a sticky real wage, employment will bear the brunt of the fluctuations in real product demand, as can be seen from equation (16). Indeed, differentiating (16) with respect to θ and L given ω, one can obtain

$$\frac{dL}{d\theta} = \frac{(\Phi + \alpha) f(.)}{\Phi \theta L \left[\frac{(1-\alpha)f(.)}{L^2} - \frac{f''(.)}{\Phi} \right]} > 0$$

Thus a decrease in the value of θ (a worsening in the real product demand) will result a fall in the employment level. In terms of the diagrammatic exposition employed by MacDonald and Solow (1981, p. 908), a decrease in the value of θ will shift both the contract curve and the power locus leftwards. So the shifts operate in the same direction as far as employment is concerned, but they operate in opposite directions as far as the negotiated wage is concerned. Therefore, employment will fall and the bargained wage rate will remain unchanged. On the other hand, changes in the values of α, Φ and χ will change the bargained real wage. One can expect the bargained wage to be negatively related to the elasticity of the production function, α, and positively related to union power, Φ, and layoff pay, χ, that is

$$\omega = \omega\,(\underset{-}{\alpha}\quad \underset{+}{\Phi}\quad \underset{+}{\chi})\tag{17}$$

This relationship requires the partial derivative of ϵ with respect to ω, denoted ϵ_ω, to be negative, i.e.

$$\epsilon_\omega = \frac{u'(\omega)}{u(\omega) - u(\chi)}\quad (1\text{-}r\text{-}\epsilon) < 0\tag{18}$$

where r is a measure of the Arrow-Pratt relative risk aversion and is defined as

$$r = -\frac{\omega u''(\omega)}{u'(\omega)}\tag{19}$$

Inequality (18) holds in the case of a risk-averse worker, i.e. $u''(\omega) < 0$ and $r > 0$, since in equilibrium $\epsilon > 1$, as can be seen from (13). In the special case of a risk-neutral worker, i.e. $u(\omega) = \omega$ and $r = 0$, inequality (18) also holds since in this case

$$\epsilon = \frac{\omega}{\omega - \chi}\quad > 1$$

We may explore further the efficient bargains model by considering the value of the bargained wage at each of the extremes values of the bargaining power parameter, Φ. If the union is powerless, i.e. $\Phi = 0$, then (13) implies that

$$\epsilon \equiv \frac{\omega u'(\omega)}{u(\omega) - u(\chi)}\quad \rightarrow \infty$$

which, in turn, implies $\omega = \chi$. In other words the real wage is equal to the real layoff pay. In terms of Figure 4.5 the power locus coincides with the labour demand curve. Hence the intersection of two loci is at point A. Since the isoprofit curve that passes through point A is the isoprofit curve of maximum profits, a powerless union will accept the real layoff pay. On the other hand, an all-powerful union will force the firm to operate along its zero isoprofit curve, since, when $\Phi \rightarrow \infty$, the power locus is given by

$$\omega = \frac{f(L)}{L}$$

Hence, the firm's real profits are zero. In terms of Figure 4.5 the intersection of the two loci is at point B. The real wage in this case is given by

$$\epsilon = \frac{1}{1 - \alpha}$$

We may close this section with an example. Let the utility function $u(\omega)$ be a constant relative risk-aversion function given by

$$u(\omega) = \frac{\omega^{1-r}}{1 - r} \ , \ r \geqslant 0$$

Let also the production function be Cobb-Douglas, i.e.

$$f(L) = k \ \theta \ \ell^{\alpha} \ ,$$

where k is a constant and $0 < \theta$ and $0 < \alpha < 1$.

The elasticity of the excess utility from work is

$$\epsilon \equiv \frac{\omega(1-r)}{\omega^r \ (\omega^{1-r} - \chi^{1-r})}$$

The contract curve is

$$\frac{\omega(1-r)}{\omega^r \ (\omega^{1-r} - \chi^{1-r})} = \frac{\omega}{\omega - \alpha \, k \, \theta \, \ell^{\alpha-1}}$$

The power locus is

$$\omega = \frac{\Phi + \alpha}{1 + \Phi} \ k \, \theta \, \ell^{\alpha-1}$$

The bargained real wage is given by

$$\frac{\omega(1-r)}{\omega^r \ (\omega^{1-r} - \chi^{1-r})} = \frac{\Phi + \alpha}{\Phi(1-\alpha)}$$

To see that the bargained wage is a mark-up on the layoff income χ, let us consider a risk neutral worker, i.e. $r = 0$. Substituting in the above equation we have

$$\frac{\omega - \chi}{\omega} = \frac{1-\alpha}{1+\alpha/\Phi}$$

The higher the union power, Φ, the higher the bargained wage over and above the layoff income χ. In the limit, an all-powerful union will force the firm to operate along its zero isoprofit curve and the bargained wage will be $\omega = \chi/\alpha$.

The employment level is

$$\ell = \left(\frac{(\Phi+1)\omega}{(\alpha+\Phi)\, k\, \theta} \right)^{\frac{1}{(\alpha-1)}}$$

3   The Efficient Bargains Model in an Open Economy

In this section we extend the efficient bargains model to the case of an open economy with a flexible exchange rate. Like in the other chapters, in the open-economy case one has to distinguish between the consumer price index and the producer price index (the GDP deflator). The consumer price index is given by

$$P_c = P^\lambda (EP^*)^{1-\lambda}, \qquad \tfrac{1}{2} < \lambda < 0$$

where

P^* is the foreign price level

E is the nominal exchange rate (defined as units of domestic currency per unit of foreign currency)

λ is the share of domestic goods in total domestic consumption. The assumption that $\tfrac{1}{2} < \lambda < 0$ means that home residents have a preference for home goods.

Let also

$$\omega^C \equiv \frac{W}{P_C} \quad \text{be the real consumer wage}$$

$$\omega^P \equiv \frac{W}{P} \quad \text{be the real producer wage}$$

and

$$\chi^C \equiv \frac{X}{P_C} \quad \text{be the real consumption layoff pay}$$

The Nash product to be maximised is

$$N = \left\{ \frac{L}{L_0} \left[u(\omega^C) - U(\chi^C) \right] \right\}^{\frac{\Phi}{1+\Phi}} \left[f(L) - \omega^P L \right]^{\frac{1}{1+\Phi}} \tag{20}$$

That is, the union is concerned with the utility of its median member derived from the real consumer wage and the firm is concerned with the real producer profit. Differentiation of (20) with respect to w and L gives the first-order conditions:

$$\tilde{\epsilon} = \frac{\omega^P}{\omega^P - f'(.)} \quad \text{(contract-curve)} \tag{21}$$

and

$$\omega^P = \frac{1}{1+\Phi} \left[\frac{\Phi f(L)}{L} + f'(L) \right] \quad \text{(power locus)} \tag{22}$$

where

$$\epsilon \equiv \frac{\omega^C u'(\omega^C)}{u(\omega^C) - u(\chi^C)} \quad \text{is the real consumer wage elasticity of net utility from work.}$$

Substituting (22) into (21) we get the bargained nominal wage, W*, given by the condition

$$\tilde{\epsilon} = \frac{\Phi + \alpha}{\Phi(1-\alpha)} \tag{23}$$

Using the definitions of $\tilde{\epsilon}$, ω^c and χ^c we may rewrite (23) as

$$\frac{\frac{W}{P_c} u'(\frac{W}{P_c})}{u(\frac{W}{P_c}) - u(\frac{X}{P_c})} = \frac{\Phi + \alpha}{\Phi(1-\alpha)} \tag{24}$$

As can be seen from (24), the nominal wage, W, is linearly homogeneous in the consumer price index and the nominal layoff pay: equiproportional increases in P_c and X will raise W in the same proportion and hence the real consumer wage will remain unchanged. However, if the nominal layoff pay is fixed, then a rise in the consumer price index will result in a less than proportional increase in the nominal wage and the real consumer wage will fall. In what follows we shall assume that the real layoff pay is unaffected by changes in the consumer price index.

Let us now examine the effects of an increase in the real exchange rate on the bargained nominal wage, W*, and the level of employment, L. For this purpose, we set $\psi = (\varphi + \alpha) / \varphi(1-\alpha)$ and we rewrite (23) as

$$\tilde{\epsilon} = \psi \tag{25}$$

We may also write the consumer price index as

$$P_c = P S^{(1-\lambda)} \tag{26}$$

where

$$S \equiv \frac{P^* E}{P} \quad \text{is the real exchange rate}$$

Let $W^* = W(P,S,\chi)$ be the solution to (25). Substituting W* into (25) we get the identity

$$\tilde{\epsilon}(W^*(P,S,\chi), P,S,\chi) = \psi(W^*(P,S,\chi)) \tag{27}$$

Differentiating (27) with respect to S we get

$$W^*_s \, (\tilde{\epsilon}_w{}^* - \psi_w{}^*) = -\tilde{\epsilon}_s \qquad (28)$$

where subscripts are used to denote derivatives of upper case letters, i.e. $W^*_s \equiv dW^*/dS$ and so on.

The expression $(\tilde{\epsilon}_w{}^* - \psi_w{}^*)$ in (28) will be negative provided that the second-order condition is satisfied. Hence the sign of W^*_s is given by the sign of $\tilde{\epsilon}_s$. From the definition of $\tilde{\epsilon}$ given above we have that

$$\tilde{\epsilon}_s = \tilde{\epsilon}_{\omega^c} \, \frac{d\omega^c}{dS} > 0 \qquad (29)$$
$$\;\;\;\;(-)\;\;\;\;(-)$$

As we have seen in section 2, the elasticity of the utility function with respect to real take-home income, $\tilde{\epsilon}_{\omega^c}$, has to be negative for a conventional relationship between the bargained wage and the parameters Φ, α and χ as described by (17). Also the sign of the derivative of the real consumer wage with respect to real exchange rate is negative:

$$\frac{d\omega^c}{dS} = -\frac{(1-\lambda)\,\omega^c}{S} < 0$$

Therefore, we have that $W^*_s > 0$, suggesting that, other things being equal, an increase in the real exchange rate, by reducing the purchasing power of workers, will lead to an increase in the bargained nominal wage, so that their real consumption wage will remain unchanged. Once more, things can be much easier by assuming a risk neutral worker, in which case the real consumption wage as a mark-up on the layoff income given by equation (25) can be rewritten as

$$\frac{\omega^c - \chi}{\omega^c} = \frac{\Phi(1-\alpha)}{\Phi+\alpha} \equiv \frac{1}{\psi} < 1$$

Hence

$$\omega^c = (\psi/\psi\text{-}1)\,\chi \text{ or } \omega P = S^{(1-\lambda)}\,(\psi/\psi\text{-}1)\,\chi$$

Thus, an increases in S will result an increase in ωP.

The next question to consider is the effect of an increase in the real exchange rate on the level of employment. Inspection of the power locus, given by (22), reveals that the employment level depends on the real product wage. At fixed domestic prices, the increase in the bargained nominal wage will result in an increase in the real producer wage which in turn will lead to a lower employment. Formally, differentiation of (22) with respect to W* gives:

$$\frac{dL}{dW^*} = \frac{(\Phi+1)}{\Phi P \left[\frac{(\alpha-1)f(.)}{L^2} + \frac{f''(.)}{\Phi} \right]} < 0$$

In terms of Figure 4.5, an increase in S will shift the contract curve leftwards (not shown) along the power locus, thus leading to a higher real product wage and lower employment.

4   Efficient Bargains, Insider Power and International Migration

In our analysis so far we have examined the efficient bargains model in the case of a closed and an open economy but we have ignored the possibility of international migration. In this section we open up the economy to international migration and we consider the efficient bargains model in a dynamic context.

As Bhagwati and Rodriguez (1983, p. 209) note, international migration in a dynamic context can be analysed either as a once-and-for-all labour movement or as a rate of migration per unit of time. Here, for simplicity, we shall treat IML as a once-and-for-all labour movement. Moreover, following Layard, Nickell and Jackman (1991), we shall start our analysis by considering the economy in an initial period where no labour outflows occur and an efficient bargains' real wage has been established. Then, we shall move on to the next period where migration outflows will be assumed to take place and we shall examine their implications for real wages and employment. More specifically, we shall consider two periods of time, period 1 and period 2. In period 1, no migration outflows take place and the labour market is described by our analysis in section 2. In period 2, which is analysed in this section, a once-and-for-all migration outflow occurs and we examine its implications for the bargained real wage and the employment level. This simplified assumption of two periods will allow us to distinguish between the two situations, i.e. no migration and migration. It may be justified on the grounds that an economy first establishes its wages and employment level, for any given international economic conditions, and then any changes in the international economic conditions are taken into account.

Since in this section we open up the economy to international migration, we need to consider first how a migration outflow will affect the bargaining between the two players, i.e. the firm and the union. To simplify the analysis we shall make the assumption that only employed workers are migrating. As will become evident shortly, because the bargained wage is determined solely by the behaviour of employed workers, whether or not the unemployed workers migrate abroad has no impact on the bargained wage.

For the firm a migration outflow will mean a lower number of employees, while for the union it will mean lower membership. At an unchanged bargained wage, lower employment will mean a lower wage bill and thus higher profits for the firm. In terms of Figure 4.5, this is illustrated by a move to a lower isoprofit curve. On the other hand, lower union membership will, at an unchanged bargained wage, increase the probability of the median member to be employed. Thus if the union is to remain on the same indifference curve the real bargained wage has to increase. Otherwise, migration outflows will move the union to a lower indifference curve. Therefore, a migration outflow will be in favour of the firm and against the union. How will the union react to this situation? Will the union bargain for higher wages or/and higher employment? To answer these questions, we need to extend the efficient bargains model to the case where the membership of the union is not fixed. The best known approach to a changing union membership is the 'insiders-outsiders model'.[1]

The insider-outsider approach was developed in a series of contributions by Lindbeck and Snower (1986, 1987), Blanchard and Summers (1986), Carruth and Oswald (1987), Gottfries and Horn (1987), Blanchard and Fischer (1989), Drazen and Gottfries (1990) and Layard, Nickell and Jackman (1991). Following the insider-outsider theory we distinguish between two types of workers: the employed trade union members, the 'insiders'; and the unemployed nonunion members, the 'outsiders'. An insider who loses his job is assumed to leave the union and to become an outsider. As a result, the trade union reflects the interest of the insiders to the detriment of the outsiders. Outsiders have no role in the bargaining process, since they are assumed not to be able to undercut employed workers. This assumption is a crucial one and is based on the existence of labour turnover costs. That is, the basic idea is that it will be costly for a firm to exchange employed union members (insiders) for unemployed union members (outsiders) because of firing and hiring costs. These labour turnover costs place a market power into the hands of the insiders, which they may exploit for their own interests, i.e. to push up their wages or to maintain their jobs. Furthermore, by reflecting the interests of the currently employed workers, the union will attach no importance to creating employment for the currently unemployed. In other words, the union's indifference curves will be kinked at an employment level equal to its current membership. Indeed, as Carlin and Soskice (1990, p. 209) argue, the objectives of the insiders are

> (1) to maintain their own employment; (2) to increase their real wage, with objective (1) taking precedence over (2); and (3) to attach no importance to creating employment for those who are currently unemployed ...

Let us assume that in period 1 the intersection of the contract curve with the power locus determines the bargained real product wage and the employment level, i.e. the point (ω_1^{p*}, L_1^*). Since the initial membership of the union was L_0, the number of unemployed union members in period 1 is given by the difference $L_0 - L_1^*$. We may now move on to period 2 and ask what will happen to union membership in this period.

Following the insiders-outsiders theory and assuming first that no migration outflows take place, union membership will be L_1^*. This means that the union's indifference curves will now be kinked at the employment (membership) level L_1^* and not at L_0. This is illustrated in Figure 4.6, where the zone of horizontal parts of the indifference curves is extended leftwards to L_1^*. That is, for $L > L_1^*$, the union reflecting the interests of the insiders will not be prepared to bear any sacrifice in wages in return for a higher level of employment. Let E denote the point with coordinates (ω_1^{p*}, L_1^*). Since the indifference curves are kinked at $L = L_1^*$ and are negatively sloping for $L < L_1^*$, the new contract curve will be positively sloped for $L < L_1^*$ and vertical at $L = L_1^*$. This is depicted in Figure 4.6 , where the new contract curve is shown by the kinked curve AEH.

We turn next our attention to the power locus. The slope and the shape of the PL is unaffected by the position of the point where the indifference curves are kinked. However, the effective part of the power locus is now CE since the union is not prepared to trade wages for employment beyond L_1^*. The intersection of the two loci will occur at point E where $\omega_2^p = \omega_1^p$ and $L_2 = L_1^*$. That is, the bargained real wage and the level of employment will be the same as in period 1, although the union membership is lower than in period 1. The reason for this is that union membership requires workers to remain employed. Therefore, the insiders of period 1, acting through their union, will bargain for a wage in period 2 such that they will not lose their insider status, i.e. maintain their jobs.

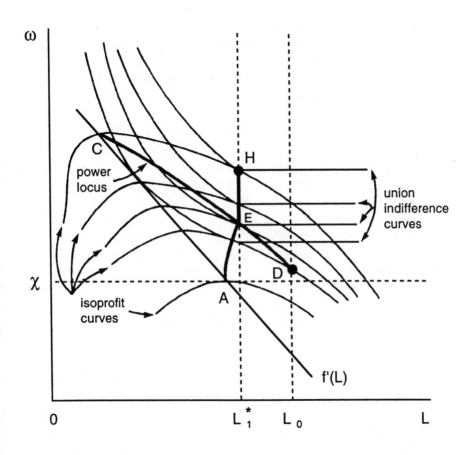

**Figure 4.6   Efficient bargains, insider power and the joint
determination of real wage and employment level**

Consider, next, the case where a migration outflow of workers occurs in period 2. What are the predictions of the efficient bargains model? What will be the bargained wage and the level of employment when firms and unions operate under conditions of international labour migration? As we have already explained at the beginning of this section, at an unchanged real wage, migration outflows will be against the welfare of the union. Therefore, the trade union has to take into account migration outflows when it bargains for real wages and employment with the firm. This, however, gives rise to the question of how migration outflows are determined and whether they are treated by the union as exogenously or are endogenously determined as the outcome of the bargain.

The case of exogenous labour outflows, in the form of a fixed quit rate per period of time, has been examined by Layard, Nickell and Jackman (1991). In their analysis, they show that the remaining insiders will achieve a higher real bargained wage. In our analysis in the previous chapters we have treated international migration as endogenously determined rather than as a fixed exogenous outflow of labour, unrelated to the existing conditions in the domestic labour market. Here we shall extend the analysis of the efficient bargains to the case of an endogenously induced outflow of labour. At this point, we make three assumptions: first, that migration outflows depend upon the bargained real wage; second, the trade union knows the size of migration outflows that may result at each level of the bargained real wage; and third, the trade union takes into account migration outflows when it bargains with the firm over real wages and employment.

Next we need to examine the behaviour of the insiders who are potential migrants. Like in the previous chapters we shall assume that the decision to migrate or not is based on the existing real consumer wage differentials between the home country and the rest of the world. Let μ denote a once-and-for-all fixed real migration cost.[2] Most of the literature on international migration, including McCulloch and Yellen (1975), Baldwin and Venables (1993), and Burda (1993)), assumes that the migration cost is fixed and the same for all migrants. However, as pointed out by the literature on search models with learning and migration,[3] the migration cost, μ, may be viewed not merely as the transportation cost, but also as a cost affected by a variety of factors, such as language and cultural differences and the existence of friends and relatives who have migrated earlier. These factors, by limiting the flow of information for some people or providing access to more information for some others, will affect μ differently across workers.[4] Therefore, we shall assume that μ is fixed for each individual but varies among migrants and that it is uniformly distributed in the interval $(0, \bar{\mu})$, where $\bar{\mu}$ is the highest migration cost. This assumption, which is commonly used in industrial organisation;[5] allows us to take account of the heterogeneity of the population concerning migration decisions.

Let ω^f be the real consumer wage in the rest of the world, which, when converted in units of domestic good, is[6]

$$\omega = \omega^f S^\lambda \tag{30}$$

where S is the real exchange rate.

The existing wage differential in period 2 between the home country and the rest of the world is $\omega - \omega_2^c$. An insider will be indifferent between migrating abroad or staying home if[7]

$$\bar{\omega} - \omega_2^c = \mu \tag{31}$$

Let $\mu^* (\omega_2^c)$ be the value of the migration cost corresponding to the marginal migrant. Then, an insider who has a migrating cost lower than μ^* (ω_2^c) will migrate while an insider with a migrating cost higher than $\mu^* (\omega_2^c)$ will stay in the home country. We may illustrate this by using the uniform distribution:

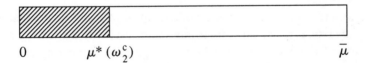

$$0 \qquad\qquad \mu^* (\omega_2^c) \qquad\qquad\qquad\qquad \bar{\mu}$$

Figure 4.7 Effective trade union membership under international migration

The whole area of the rectangle represents union membership in period 1 (insiders), which is split up by the migration cost $\mu^* (\omega_2^c)$. The number of migrants is given by the number of workers whose migration cost is in the interval $[0, \mu^* (\omega_2^c))$, shown by the shadowed rectangular area in Figure 4.7. The remaining part of the rectangle shows the number of non-migrating insiders and hence the effective membership of the union in period 2. Therefore, the outflow of workers in period 2 is given by

$$\frac{\mu^* (.)}{\bar{\mu}} L_1^* = \frac{\bar{\omega} - \omega_2^c}{\bar{\mu}} L_1^* \tag{32}$$

The Union

As we have assumed earlier, the union of insiders takes into account migration outflows when it bargains with the firm. Therefore, in period 2, the union's effective membership[8] denoted by M_2^e, will be

$$M_2^e = L_1^* - \frac{\bar{\omega} - \omega_2^c}{\bar{\mu}} L_1^* = L_1^* (1 - \frac{\bar{\omega} - \omega_2^c}{\bar{\mu}}) \tag{33}$$

Obviously

$$M_2^e = L_1^* \text{ as long as } \bar{\omega} = \omega_2^c$$

and

$$M_2^e < L_1^* \text{ as long as } 0 < \omega - \omega_2^c < \bar{\mu}.$$

That is, in the absence of a real wage differential between the home country and the rest of the world, the effective union membership will be equal to the first period's employment level. In the presence of wage differentials, however, the effective membership in period 2 will be lower than the employment of the first period.

Furthermore, the effective membership is an increasing function of the real wage rate, ω_2^c, and the average migrating cost ($\bar{\mu}/2$), while it is a decreasing function of the rest of the world real wage rate, $\bar{\omega}$, measured in domestic currency units. That is, an increase in the average migration cost will reduce the percentage of migrating insiders. An increase in the real domestic consumer wage, by lowering the wage differential will induce a lower number of insiders to migrate. Finally, an increase in $\bar{\omega}$ due to an increase in ω^f or an increase in S, by widening the wage differential, will induce a larger number of insiders to migrate.

The effective union membership can be illustrated in Figure 4.8 in the (w^p, L) space by the upwards sloping line MΛ.

We may now turn our analysis to the trade union. How will the union act when it is faced with the possibility that its members may migrate abroad? Given that the union is assumed to care about the welfare of its existing employed members, the kink of the union's indifference curves will occur along its effective membership line MΛ. That is, the union's indifference curves will be horizontal to the right of the membership line ML and

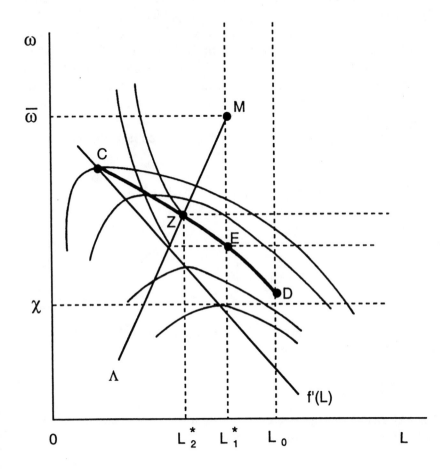

Figure 4.8 **Effective trade union membership and the joint determination of real wage and employment level under international migration**

downwards sloping to the left of it. Furthermore, since we are to the right of
the demand curve, the points of tangency between an isoprofit curve and a
union's indifference curves are along the MΛ line. That is, in period 2, the
effective membership line MΛ is now the new contract curve. Efficient bargains
in period 2 are therefore on the MΛ line. The particular point of the MΛ line
that will determine the bargained real wage and the level of employment is
given by the intersection of the MΛ with the power locus CE. Let Z be the
point of intersection. At Z the bargained wage is higher than at E, since a
movement from E to Z, along the downward sloping power locus, represents
higher wages and lower employment. Algebraically, point Z is determined by
the solution to the equation for effective membership, given by (33), and by
the expression for the power locus which is obtained from the maximisation
of

$$
\underset{L}{\text{Max}} \left[\frac{L}{M_2^e} \left[U(\omega \tfrac{c}{2}) - U(\chi) \right] \right]^{\frac{\Phi}{1+\Phi}} \left[f(L) - \omega^P L \right]^{\frac{1}{1+\Phi}}
\tag{34}
$$

That is,

$$
\omega \tfrac{P}{2} = \frac{1}{1+\Phi} \left[\frac{\Phi f(L_2)}{L_2} + f'(L_2) \right]
\tag{35}
$$

To study the comparative statics we shall make the assumption of a Cobb-
Douglas production function i.e.

$$
f(L) = k L^{\alpha}
\tag{36}
$$

where k is a constant and $0 < \alpha < 1$. Substituting (36) into the equation for the
power locus and solving for L_2 we obtain

$$
L_2 = b \, (\omega \tfrac{P}{2})^{-\frac{1}{1-\alpha}}
\tag{37}
$$

where

$$
b = \left[\frac{(\alpha + \Phi)k}{(1+\Phi)} \right]^{\frac{1}{1-\alpha}} > 0
$$

Substituting (37) into the equation for the effective union membership and rearranging we have

$$b(\omega_2^p)^{-\frac{1}{1-\alpha}} - L_1^* \left[1 - \frac{\bar{\omega} - \omega_2^c}{\bar{\mu}} \right] = 0 \qquad (38)$$

Proposition 1 The home real product wage as well as the home real consumption wage will be higher under conditions of international migration than without international migration.

This is because an existing wage differential between the home country and abroad, i.e. $\bar{\omega} > \omega_2^p$, will create a migration outflow of workers and will therefore reduce the number of remaining insiders and thus the number of jobs to be protected by the union. Since the behaviour of the union is determined by the behaviour of insiders who are also assumed to be able to know the migration outflow of the union members, the union will bargain for a real wage so that all of its remaining members will be employed i.e. $M_2^e = L_2 < L_1^*$. Given the negative relationship between employment and real product wages, reflected in the power locus, the union will achieve a higher real product wage ω_2^p than that achieved in the absence of international migration, i.e $\omega_2^p > \omega_1^p$. This also implies a higher real consumption wage in period 2, i.e. $\omega_2^c > \omega_1^c$, for any given real exchange rate. Therefore, using the assumption of risk neutrality, we may write $\omega_2^c > \omega_1^c = [\psi/(\psi-1)] \chi$.

Proposition 2 Real product and real consumption wages in period 2 are inversely related to membership in period 1.

From (38) we have

$$\frac{d\omega_2^p}{dL_1^*} = \frac{(\omega_2 p)^{(1+\sigma)} S^{(1-\lambda)} (\bar{\omega} - \omega_2^c - \bar{\mu})}{b \bar{\mu} \sigma S^{(1-\lambda)} + L_1^* (\omega_2^p)^{(1+\sigma)}} < 0$$

and

$$\frac{d\omega_2^c}{dL_1^*} = \frac{(\omega_2 p)^{(1+\sigma)} (\bar{\omega} - \omega_2^c - \bar{\mu})}{b \bar{\mu} \sigma S^{(1-\lambda)} + L_1^* (\omega_2 p)^{(1+\sigma)}} < 0$$

where $\sigma = 1 / (1-\alpha)$ and $\bar{\omega} - \omega_2^c < \bar{\mu}$.

That is, for any given wage differential between the home country and abroad, higher union membership in period 1 will result in higher effective membership in period 2. Since effective membership is equal to employment in period 2, the employment level in period 2 will increase. This in turn is possible only through a lower real product wage. Therefore, higher membership in period 1 will be associated with a lower real consumption wage in period 2.

Proposition 3 An increase in the average migration cost will reduce the home real consumption wage:

$$\frac{d\omega_2^P}{d\bar{\mu}} = - \frac{(\bar{\omega} - \omega_2^c)\, L_1^* \, S^{(1-\lambda)} \, (\omega_2^P)^{(1+\sigma)}}{\bar{\mu}\, [b\, \bar{\mu}\, \sigma\, S^{(1-\lambda)} + L_1^* \, (\omega_2^P)^{(1+\sigma)}]} < 0$$

and

$$\frac{d\omega_2^c}{d\bar{\mu}} = - \frac{(\bar{\omega} - \omega_2^c)\, L_1^* \, (\omega_2^P)^{(1+\sigma)}}{\bar{\mu}\, [b\, \bar{\mu}\, \sigma\, S^{(1-\lambda)} + L_1^* \, (\omega_2^P)^{(1+\sigma)}]} < 0$$

That is, an increase in the average migration cost, by reducing the percentage of insiders who are potential migrants at any given wage differential between home and abroad, will result in a higher number of non-migrating insiders. Therefore, more jobs should be protected by the union and the bargained real product wage has to be lower at a higher average migration cost. The lower home real product wage will in turn result in a lower home real consumer wage.

Proposition 4 An increase in the rest of the world wage rate measured in foreign currency units will increase both the home real product wage and the home real consumer wage:

$$\frac{d\omega_2^P}{d\omega^f} = \frac{L_1^* \, S \, (\omega_2^P)^{(1+\sigma)}}{b\, \bar{\mu}\, \sigma\, S^{(1-\lambda)} + L_1^* \, (\omega_2^P)^{(1+\sigma)}} > 0$$

and

$$\frac{d\omega_2^c}{d\omega^f} = \frac{L_1^* \, S^{\lambda} \, (\omega_2^P)^{(1+\sigma)}}{b\, \bar{\mu}\, \sigma\, S^{(1-\lambda)} + L_1^* \, (\omega_2^P)^{(1+\sigma)}} > 0$$

That is, an increase in ω^f, by increasing the existing real wage differential between home and abroad, will induce a larger number of insiders to migrate abroad. Therefore, the remaining insiders, acting through their unions, will be able to increase the real product wage. Moreover, at a given real exchange rate, the increase in the real product wage will increase the home real consumer wage.

Proposition 5 An increase in the real exchange rate, will increase the home real product wage. The sign of the change in the home real consumer wage is ambiguous:

$$\frac{d\omega_2^P}{dS} = \frac{L_1^* (\omega_2^P)^{(1+\sigma)}[\omega^f \lambda S + (1-\lambda) \omega_2^P]}{S [b \bar{\mu} \sigma S^{(1-\lambda)} + L_1^* (\omega_2^P)^{(1+\sigma)}]} > 0$$

and

$$\frac{d\omega_2^C}{dS} = \frac{(\omega_2^P)^{(1+\sigma)} L_1^* \bar{\omega} \sigma (1-\lambda) (\xi - \eta)}{S [b \bar{\mu} \sigma S^{(1-\lambda)} + L_1^* (\omega_2^P)^{(1+\sigma)}]} \quad ?$$

where

$$\xi = 1 + \frac{\lambda (1-\alpha)}{(1-\lambda)} > 1$$

$$\eta = \frac{\bar{\mu} + \omega_2^C}{\bar{\omega}} > 1 \text{ , since } \bar{\omega} < \bar{\mu} + \omega_2^C$$

If $\xi \geqslant \eta$ then $(d\omega_2^C/dS) \geqslant 0$; otherwise $(d\omega_2^C/dS) < 0$. That is, an increase in the real exchange rate (depreciation) will increase the existing real wage differential between home and abroad through two channels. First, it will increase the real rest-of-the-world consumer wage in domestic-currency units. Second, it will reduce the home real consumption wage. The increase in the existing real wage differential will induce a larger proportion of insiders to migrate abroad. Therefore, the smaller number of remaining insiders, acting through their union, will succeed in achieving a higher real product wage. In terms of Figure 4.8, an increase in S will shift the MA line leftwards (not shown) along the power locus and will thus lead to a higher real product wage and lower employment in period 2. Moreover, whether or not the increase in real product wage will affect the home real consumption wage depends upon the value of ξ relative to that of η, which, in turn, depends upon the percentage of potential migrants, the elasticity of the production function with respect to labour and the relative share of home goods in total domestic consumption.

Proposition 6 A positive technological shock by strengthening the bargaining position of the trade union will lead to an increase in both the real consumer wage and the employment level.

As in section 1, following Blanchard and Fischer (1989), we rewrite the production function as $f(L) = k\ \theta\ L^{\alpha}$, where θ is a technological shock. A positive technological shock, by increasing both the marginal product of labour and the average product, will shift the power locus upwards along the unchanged membership line and will thus lead to a higher real product wage and employment level.

Indeed, equations (37) and (38) remain the same except that the value of b is now given by $\tilde{b} = b\theta$. Differentiating (38) with respect to θ and $d\omega_2^P$, one can obtain

$$\frac{d\omega_2^P}{d\theta} = \frac{b\ \bar{\mu}\ \sigma\ S^{(1-\lambda)}\ \theta^{\alpha\sigma}\ (\omega_2^P)^{(1+\sigma)}}{b\ \bar{\mu}\ \sigma\ S^{(1-\lambda)} + L_1{}^*\ (\omega_2^P)^{(1+\sigma)}} \quad > 0$$

and

$$\frac{d\omega_2^c}{d\theta} = \frac{\bar{b}\bar{\mu}\ \sigma\ \theta^{\alpha\sigma}\ (\omega_2^P)^{(1+\sigma)}}{b\ \bar{\mu}\ \sigma\ S^{(1-\lambda)} + L_1^*\ (\omega_2^P)^{(1+\sigma)}} \quad > 0$$

also differentiating (33) we have

$$\frac{dL_2}{d\theta} = \frac{b\ \sigma\ L_1{}^*\ \theta^{\alpha\sigma}\ (\omega_2^P)^{(1+\sigma)}}{b\ \bar{\mu}\ \sigma\ S^{(1-\lambda)} + L_1{}^*\ (\omega_2^P)^{(1+\sigma)}} \quad > 0$$

Concluding this section we may therefore write

$$\omega_2^{c*} = \omega_2\ (\bar{\omega}, L_1^*, \bar{\mu}, \theta) \text{ and } L_2^* = L_2\ (\bar{\omega}, L_1^*, \bar{\mu}, \theta)$$
$$\phantom{\omega_2^{c*} = \omega_2\ (}\text{+ -   - +}\text{- +   + +}$$

5   Conclusions

In this chapter we have incorporated the possibility of international migration of labour into a model of open economy with a non-competitive labour market. Our approach to the specification of the labour market is based on a trade union model where employed workers can exercise insider power. The model we have developed allows for a simultaneous determination of union membership and real wages under conditions of migration outflows.

In this framework, we have shown that migration outflows, by reducing the membership of the trade union, lead to a real consumer wage higher than what would have been in the absence of migration. We have also shown that an increase in the rest-of-the-world wage or a decrease in the migration cost, by inducing a larger proportion of insiders to migrate abroad, will lead to higher real consumer wages at home. An increase in the real exchange rate will also increase the home real product wage. However, the sign of change in the home real consumer wage is ambiguous. Finally, a positive technological shock, by strengthening the bargaining position of the trade union, will raise both the domestic real consumer wage and the employment level.

Notes

1   The extension of the efficient bargains model to the case insider power is quite natural since, as Layard, Nickell and Jackman, (1991) note, 'any union model of unemployment is (and always has been) a model of insider power ...'.
2   The migration cost, μ, can be treated as amortized cost, i.e. annual payments equivalent to the total lump-sum cost of emigration. See McCulloch and Yellen (1975).
3   See Johnson and Salt (1990) and Molho (1986) for a survey.
4   This derivation of migration function also allows us to derive a linear form of migration function rather than the general form we have adopted in the previous chapters.
5   See, e.g. Tirole (1988) and Booth and Chatterji (1993).
6   Note that the foreign real consumption wage in home currency purchasing-power units, $\bar{\omega}$, can be expressed as

$$\bar{\omega} = \frac{\omega^f P_c^* E}{P_c}$$

where

ω^f is the foreign real consumer wage in foreign-currency purchasing power units

P_c^* is the foreign real consumer prices in foreign-currency purchasing power units

$P_c = P^\lambda (EP^*)^{1-\lambda}$ is the home country's CPI

E is the nominal exchange rate (defined as the home currency price of foreign currency)

$S \equiv \dfrac{EP^*}{P}$ is the real exchange rate.

Using the definition of P_c and normalising P_c^* and P^* to unity we have $\bar{\omega} = \omega^f S^\lambda$.

7   We have made the assumption of risk neutral workers in order to simplify our analysis. This assumption is commonly used in the international migration literature (see, for example, Bhagwati and Hamada (1974, 1975) and McCulloch and Yellen (1975). The case of a risk aversion utility will complicate our analysis without changing our results.

8   This can be seen as a membership demand. See Booth and Chatterji (1993) for a similar derivation but in a framework that ignores insider power and migration.

5 International Migration of Labour and Monetary Policy Games

1 Introduction

In the previous chapter we examined the effects of international migration in the context of an efficient-bargains trade union model where a representative union and a firm were bargaining over the joint determination of the wage rate and the level of employment. In this analysis we ignored government policy by implicitly assuming that either the government played a passive role or policy variables remained unchanged. Obviously, governments do not play a passive role: they have their own objectives with respect to unemployment and inflation and these objectives are affected by trade unions' choices. Indeed, trade union behaviour often motivates government actions. Similarly, government actions affect the unions' objectives and rational trade union behaviour implies that government actions have to be taken into account. Within this framework of actions and counteractions by trade unions and the government, economic policy and wage formation need to be analysed as a two-player game.

This chapter incorporates the possibility of international migration into a simple monetary policy game between governments and trade unions. The game-theoretic approach to macroeconomic policy in open economies has been expanding rapidly in recent years: see e.g. Rogoff (1985), Gylfanson and Lindbeck (1986, 1991), Canzoneri and Henderson (1988), Driffill and Schultz (1992), Zervoyianni (1993) and Jensen (1993a,b).[1] However, macroeconomic policy games have been analysed within the context of models in which the labour force is fixed. In the model we present and analyse in this chapter we distinguish between the initial labour force, which is given exogenously, and the effective labour force, which depends on the rate of labour migration. Like in the previous chapters, international migration is assumed to be generated by an existing real-consumption-wage differential

143

between the home country and the rest of the world. Because real consumption wages depend on nominal wages and on nominal money supplies, the size of migration flows, and thus the size of the effective labour force, also depends on the actions of the two 'players', i.e. the union and the government. Since changes in the effective labour force will affect unemployment levels, they will also affect the objectives of both players. In effect, the presence of international migration implies additional interactions between the two players.

Our analysis in this chapter thus has two objectives. The first is to establish the implications of international migration for the outcomes of non-cooperative and cooperative games played by governments and trade unions in open economies. The second objective of the analysis is to explore whether international migration has any impact on the results already established by the recent game-theoretic international macro-literature that assumes a non-migrating labour force.

The chapter is organised as follows. Section 2 considers a small open economy that takes all foreign variables as given. Following, e.g. Gylfanson and Lindbeck (1986), Hersoug (1986), Driffill and Schultz (1992) and Cubit (1992), we assume that the entire domestic labour force is organised in a single all embracing monopoly union which sets nominal wages unilaterally with a view to maximising a utility function defined in terms of real consumption wages and employment. Wage contracts are for one period: at the end of each period, unions and firms are assumed to sign contracts that specify nominal wages and employment rules for the following period, see also Zervoyianni (1993) and Alogoskoufis (1994). On the other hand, policy-makers set the money supply at the beginning of each period with a view to maximising a macro welfare function defined over home employment and consumer price index (CPI) inflation. Both a non-cooperative and a cooperative game between the union and the policy-makers are considered, first in the case of no migration and then under conditions of international migration.

Under no migration, a non-cooperative regime is found to lead to relatively high real wages and a non-zero rate of inflation. A cooperative regime leads to a relatively low level of unemployment and zero rate of CPI inflation. As a result, policy-makers are better off under cooperation. By contrast the trade union is better off under the non-cooperative regime. International migration does not affect the relative desirability of the two regimes from the point of view of each player. However, it does improve the absolute position of each player in each regime and thus it constitutes a Pareto improvement relative to the non-migration situation. This is because, by affecting domestic unemployment through its impact on the domestic effective labour force and having no effect on CPI inflation, international migration creates a positive externality for both players and hence it improves their welfare

In section 3 we extend the model developed in section 2 to the case of two interdependent economies. In an interdependent world, policies in one country affect macroeconomic aggregates in other countries and so national policy-makers are engaged in a strategic interplay. Following, for example, Rogoff (1985), Canzoneri and Henderson (1988), Zervoyianni (1993) and Jensen (1993a,b) we consider two regimes for the policy-makers: they may behave as non-cooperative players or they may cooperate. On the other hand, we assume that unions cooperate neither between themselves nor with the policy makers.

The analysis shows that Rogoff's (1985) conclusion that monetary policies are more expansionary when policy-makers cooperate than when they do not cooperate does not necessarily hold under conditions of international migration. The reason is that in a non-cooperative regime, the presence of international migration allows each policy-maker to exercise an additional positive influence on unemployment by increasing the money supply: an increase in the domestic money supply relative to the foreign money supply, lowers the effective labour force of the country where the monetary expansion occurs by inducing migration flows through its impact on the real wage differentials. In a non-cooperative regime, each policy-maker will, therefore, choose a relatively more expansionary monetary policy. By contrast, in a cooperative regime each policy-maker knows that any attempt to induce a drop in his country's effective labour force through migration flows will be offset by equal attempts abroad. As a result, each policy-maker's incentive to use monetary policy to reduce unemployment is relatively weaker. Accordingly, whether monetary policies will be more expansionary under cooperation than under non-cooperation will depend upon the relative size of two opposing externalities: the negative externality arising from the real-exchange-rate effect on CPIs of unilateral monetary expansions; and the positive externality arising from the impact of these expansions on the effective labour force through international migration. If the welfare effect of the positive externality dominates, then cooperation between home and foreign policy-makers will lead to a Pareto improvement relative to a non-cooperative regime and inter-government cooperation in the monetary field will turn out to be advantageous.

2   Monetary Policy Games in a Small Open Economy with International Migration

We consider a small open economy with a flexible exchange rate which operates under conditions of international migration.[2] Like in the previous chapters, international migration is assumed to be generated by a real wage differential between the home country and the rest of the world. In particular, a real wage differential against the home country is assumed to lead to a labour flow from the home country to the rest of the world. As a result, the effective labour force of the home country, denoted by n_0, depends on the rate of migration and thus on the size of the real-consumption-wage differential.

Therefore, the (log of the) effective labour force, can be specified as:

$$n_0 = \ell_0 - \sigma (w_c^f - w_c^* - \mu), \qquad \sigma > 0 \qquad (1a)$$

where

ℓ_0 is the domestic labour force in the absence of labour migration
σ is a migration parameter
$w_c^f \equiv w_c^* + (1-h)z^e$ is the expected foreign real consumption wage in home currency purchasing-power units[3] with $0 < h < \frac{1}{2}$
w_c^* is the foreign real consumer wage in foreign-currency purchasing-power units
$z \equiv e - p + p^*$ is the real exchange rate
e is the nominal exchange rate (defined as the home currency price of foreign currency)
p, p^* are the prices of home and foreign outputs respectively
w_c^e is the (expected) real consumption wage at home
μ is a once-and-for-all migration cost

Equation (1) says that under conditions of international migration ($\sigma \neq 0$), one has to distinguish between the exogenously given labour force ℓ_0 and the effective labour force n_0. Using the definition of w_c^f we can write (1a) as

$$n_0 = \ell_0 - \sigma [w_c^* + (1-h)z^e - w_c^* - \mu] \qquad (1b)$$

That is, an increase in the (expected) home real consumption wage or in migration costs will increase the domestic effective labour force. On the other hand, increases in w_c^* or z will, other things being equal, lead to a lower n_0.

The rest of the model is similar to those in Canzoneri and Henderson (1988), Zervoyianni (1993) and Jensen (1993a,b). We assume that the home country produces a homogeneous product that is an imperfect substitute in consumption for imports. The production of this product is carried out by perfectly competitive firms which maximise profits. Accordingly, assuming Cobb-Douglas production functions and taking capital to be fixed, output is an increasing function of employment, n,

$$y = vn + v_0, \qquad 0 < v < 1, \qquad v_0 > 0, \qquad (2)$$

and profit maximisation implies a labour-demand function of the form:

$$n = -(1-v)^{-1} (w-p) + v_1, \qquad v_1 > 0 \qquad (3)$$

The home labour force is assumed to be organised in a single union. The union decides nominal wages unilaterally, and we assume that wage rates are set only at regular intervals. This means that the union always has to act on the expectation of the policy-maker's behaviour, since money supplies can be changed by the policy-makers at any time. Thus, the union sets nominal wages for every period t on the basis of all information available at the end of period t-l. Along the lines suggested, for example, by Driffill (1985) and Jensen (1993a, b), we assume that nominal wages are set so as to maximise a utility function of the form

$$U = -(n^e - n^e{}_0)^2 + bw_c{}^e, \qquad b > 0 \qquad (4)$$

where b reflects the relative weight assigned by the union to real consumer wage versus employment. Equation (4) says that the union dislikes deviations of employment from 'full employment' and that, for a given level of employment, it aims at as high a real consumer wage as possible.

The real consumption wage is

$$w_c = w - q \qquad (5)$$

where w is the nominal wage rate and q denotes the consumer price index (CPI). The CPI is a weighted average of the price of domestic output and the domestic-currency price of imports:

$$q = (1-h)p + h(e+p^*), \qquad 0 < h < \tfrac{1}{2} \qquad (6a)$$

where h is the share of imported goods in total domestic consumption. The assumption that $0 < h < \frac{1}{2}$ means that home residents have a preference for home goods. Using the definition of the real exchange rate, we may rewrite (6a) as:

$$q = p + hz \tag{6b}$$

Aggregate demand for domestic output, is positively related to the real exchange rate:[4]

$$y = sz \tag{7}$$

As far as home policy-makers are concerned, their control variable is the money supply which they choose at the beginning of every time period t so as to maximise a 'social welfare' function defined over home employment and CPI inflation of the form:

$$V = -(n-n_0)^2 - c(q-q_{-1})^2, \quad c > 0 \tag{8a}$$

(8a) says that policy-makers dislike changes in the consumer price index since price instability entails cost to all economic agents. Policy-makers also dislike deviations of the actual level of employment from its 'full-employment' level, i.e. the effective home labour force n_0. The parameter c is the relative weight assigned by the policy-makers to CPI inflation relative to employment. Normalising q_{-1} to zero we can rewrite (8a) as

$$V = -(n-n_0)^2 - cq^2 \tag{8b}$$

To complete the model we introduce (9) which represents the condition for equilibrium in the money market:

$$m = p + y \tag{9}$$

(9) is a simple quantity-theory equation.

Through appropriate substitutions, (2)–(9) can be reduced to six equations determining equilibrium values for the variables n, y, w_c, q, p and z as functions of the policy-makers' and the union's control variables, namely m and w:

$$n = m - w$$

$$y = v(m - w)$$

$$w_c = \frac{d}{s} (w - m)$$

$$q = v(1 - \frac{h}{s}) w + \frac{d}{s} m$$

$$p = (1 - v) m + vw$$

$$z = \frac{v}{s} (m - w) \qquad\qquad\qquad (10)$$

where $d = hv + s(1 - v) > 0$ and, for notational simplicity, all constant terms are suppressed.

Two features of (10) are worth noting. First, a monetary expansion will, other things being equal, lead to an increase in the price of domestic output and thus in q. The increase in p, by reducing the real product wage, will result in higher employment and thus higher output. The increase in domestic output will have to be followed by a real exchange rate depreciation to maintain equilibrium in the goods market. This will further increase the consumer price index. The increase in CPI will reduce the real consumer wage, w_c. On the other hand, an increase in the nominal wage rate w, by lowering employment demand, will lead to a fall in domestic output, which, in turn, will lead to an increase in p through the condition of equilibrium in the money market and to an appreciation of the real exchange rate through the goods market. These two effects of changes in w work in opposite directions in affecting the CPI. However, as long as $0 < h < \frac{1}{2}$, the first effect can be expected to dominate, i.e. $(1 - h/s) > 0$ in which case the CPI will increase. The initial increase in the nominal wage rate and the subsequent increase in CPI will affect the real consumer wage in an opposite direction, but their overall effect will be an increase in w_c.

Using (10) the effective labour force n_0 can be expressed as

$$n_0 = \ell_0 - \frac{\sigma}{s} [d + v(1 - h)] (m - w) - \sigma(w_c* - \mu) \qquad (11)$$

With a non-zero σ, the domestic effective labour force is negatively related to the domestic money supply and the foreign real consumer wage. It is positively related to the home nominal wage rate and the once-and-for-all migration cost. To explain these effects recall that at the initial equilibrium, a real wage differential is assumed to exist between the home country and the rest of the world. Accordingly, by causing a real exchange rate depreciation, an increase in m will affect the existing wage differential through two channels. First, it will raise the purchasing power of the foreign real wage w^f_c; second, it will reduce the home real consumer wage w_c. Both effects will induce domestic workers to migrate abroad and will thus result in a fall in the domestic labour force. On the other hand, an exogenous increase in the domestic nominal wage rate w, by increasing the home real consumer wage and causing a real exchange rate appreciation, will reduce the initial real wage differential. This discourages domestic workers from migrating abroad, leading to a larger domestic effective labour force. For similar reasons, an exogenous increase in the foreign real consumer wage, or a reduction in migration costs, will cause n_0 to fall.

Consider now wage setting and money-supply setting. In a Nash non-cooperative environment, the union, taking expected money supply as given, will set w to maximise (4). That is the union will solve:

$$\max_{w} U \text{ s.t (10) and } \frac{\partial m^e}{\partial w} = 0$$

This leads to the following first-order condition

$$2(n-n_0)\left[1 + \frac{\sigma}{s}\left[d + v(1 - h)\right]\right] + \frac{bd}{s} = 0,$$

which, using (10), yields the union's Nash reaction function describing its best responses to the policy-maker moves:

$$w = m^e - \frac{s}{\kappa}\ell_0 + \frac{\sigma s}{\kappa}(w_c{}^* - \mu) + \frac{bds}{2\kappa^2} \tag{12}$$

where $\kappa = s + \sigma\left[d + v(1 - h)\right] > 0$.

Under a Nash regime the home policy-maker maximises his objective function (8b) treating the union's action variable w as parametric, i.e. he will solve:

$$\max_{m} V \text{ s.t (10) and } \frac{\partial w}{\partial m} = 0$$

This leads to the following first-order condition:

$$(n-n_0) \left[1 + \frac{\sigma}{s} [d + v(1 - h)] \right] + \frac{cd}{s} q = 0$$

Using (10), one obtains the policy-maker's reaction function:

$$m = \frac{\delta_1 - cds}{\delta_1} w + \frac{\kappa s}{\delta_1} \ell_0 - \frac{\sigma \kappa s}{\delta_1} (w_c{}^* - \mu) \qquad (13)$$

where $\delta_1 = \kappa^2 + cd^2 > 0$ and also $\delta_1 - cds > 0$.

Consider the union's reaction function (12). A one unit increase in m, by increasing employment and by lowering the home effective labour force, leads to lower home unemployment. The increase in m also reduces the real consumption wage. The home union can offset the impact of the rise in m on w_c and n_0 by raising the nominal wage rate by one unit, since changes in m and w have an opposite effect on w_c and n_0 of the same magnitude. Thus, in (12) a one unit increase in m leads to an equal increase in w. The presence of international migration does not affect the size of this effect. As far as the impact of changes in the exogenously given labour force ℓ_0 on the union's reaction function (12) is concerned, we know from equation (4) that the union cares about unemployment as well as about the real consumer wage. However, a large initial labour force requires a high level of employment to keep unemployment low. Other things being equal, this can only be achieved through a low nominal wage. Hence, the nominal wage rate and the initial labour force ℓ_0 are negatively related in (12). Note that in the absence of migration, a one unit increase in ℓ_0 will be associated with a one unit fall in the nominal wage. Under conditions of international migration, on the other hand, part of the initial domestic labour force migrates abroad and thus a one unit increase in ℓ_0 results in a less than one unit fall in the nominal wage. The effects of changes in the migration cost μ and the foreign real consumer wage $w_c{}^*$ are entirely due to international migration. A one-unit increase in $w_c{}^*$, by inducing more workers to migrate abroad, will result in a lower home effective labour force. Therefore, a lower level of employment will be required to keep domestic unemployment low. For a given m and a given ℓ_0, this allows the union to set relatively high nominal wages. Therefore, higher wages abroad will result in higher nominal wages at home. Finally, the constant term in (12) captures the effect of changes in the real consumer wage on the optimal nominal wage rate: a higher real consumer wage will, other things being equal, require a higher nominal wage rate. The presence of international migration will reduce the size of this effect since a higher home real consumer wage, by reducing migration outflows, will leave the economy with a larger effective labour force and thus will induce the union to set relatively lower nominal wages.

As far as the reaction function of the home policy-maker (13) is concerned, an increase in w, by reducing employment and increasing the effective labour force through migration flows, will lead to higher domestic unemployment and also to higher CPI inflation. The rise in unemployment can be offset by an equal increase in m. On the other hand, as equation (10) shows, the adverse impact of the rise in w on the CPI can be offset by an increase in m smaller than that in w. The policy-maker's optimal strategy, then, is to increase m by a smaller amount than the rise in w so as to partially offset the impact of the nominal wage increase on both unemployment and CPI inflation. The presence of international migration increases the size of this effect, since the larger effective labour force caused by the increase in w, will require a relatively higher m to keep unemployment low. On the other hand, a large initial labour force requires a higher level of employment to maintain low unemployment. Given the positive relation between employment and the money supply this requires more expansionary monetary policy. This effect is smaller in the presence of international migration since the outflow of workers will reduce the initial labour force. Finally an increase in w_c^* (decrease in μ), by inducing migration outflows, will result in a lower effective labour force thus requiring lower money stock to maintain low unemployment.

Assuming that expectations are formed rationally, so that $m^e = m$, Nash equilibrium is obtained by combining equations (12) and (13). Solving for w and m we obtain the Nash optimum values:

$$w^N = - \frac{d}{\kappa} \ell_0 + \frac{b\delta_1}{2c\kappa^2} + \frac{d\sigma}{\kappa} (w_c^* - \mu)$$

and

$$m^N = \frac{v(s-h)}{\kappa} \ell_0 + \frac{b(\delta_1 - cds)}{2c\kappa^2} - \frac{\sigma v(s-h)}{\kappa} (w_c^* - \mu) \tag{14}$$

where $\delta_1 - cds > 0$, $\sigma v(s-h)/\kappa > 0$

Consider now equilibrium under cooperation between the two players. Behaving as cooperative players, the home union and the home policy-maker will set w and m taking into account the impact of their actions on each other. The home union will thus choose w with a view to maximising the value of a welfare function of the form $uv(.) = (1 - \tau) U + \tau V^e$, which is a weighted sum of its own utility function and the (expected) value of the home policy-maker's objective function (see e.g. Zervoyianni (1993)). Making the simplifying assumption that $\tau = \frac{1}{2}$, we obtain the first-order condition:

$$2(n-n_0)\left[1 + \frac{\sigma[d + v(1-h)]}{s}\right] + \frac{bd}{2s} - \frac{v(s-h)c}{s}\, q = 0$$

Using (10) and solving for w, we have:

$$w^C = \frac{2\kappa^2 + cd(d-s)}{\theta_1}\, m^e - \frac{2\kappa s}{\theta_1}\, \ell_0 + \frac{2\kappa s\sigma}{\theta_1}\,(w_c^* - \mu) + \frac{bds}{2\theta_1} \qquad (15a)$$

where $\theta_1 = 2\kappa^2 + c(d-s)^2 > 0$.

On the other hand, the policy-maker will choose m with a view to maximising the value of a welfare function of the form $vu(.) = (1 - \lambda) V + \lambda U$, where λ is the relative weight placed by the policy-maker on the utility of the union (see also Zervoyianni, 1993). Assuming equal weights, we obtain the following first-order condition:

$$2(n-n_0)\left[1 + \frac{\sigma[d + v(1-h)]}{s}\right] - \frac{bd}{2s} + \frac{cd}{s}\, q = 0$$

Using (10) and solving for m we have

$$m^C = \frac{2\kappa^2 + cd(d-s)}{\theta_2}\, w - \frac{2\kappa s}{\theta_2}\, \ell_0 - \frac{2\kappa s\sigma}{\theta_2}\,(w_c^* - \mu) - \frac{bds}{2\theta_2} \qquad (15b)$$

where $\theta_2 = 2\kappa^2 + cd^2$.

With $m^e = m$, (15a) and (15b) yield the following equilibrium values for w and m:

$$w^C = -\frac{d}{\kappa}\, \ell_0 + \frac{bd^2}{4\kappa^2} + \frac{d\sigma}{\kappa}\,(w_c^* - \mu)$$

$$m^C = \frac{v(s-h)}{\kappa}\, \ell_0 - \frac{bd(s-d)}{4\kappa^2} - \frac{\sigma v(s-h)}{\kappa}\,(w_c^* - \mu) \qquad (16)$$

Let us compare the cooperative regime and the non-cooperative regime in terms of the equilibrium nominal wage rate and the money supply. From equations (14) and (16) it is apparent that non-cooperation leads the union to choose relatively high nominal wages. The reason for this is straightforward:

in the non-cooperative regime the union sets nominal wages without taking into account the effect of its actions on the policy-makers' objectives. Thus, the union will base its decisions on the fact that an increase in the nominal wage w will have a positive effect on the real wages but it will also have a negative effect on unemployment. On the other hand, when the two players cooperate the union takes explicitly into account that in addition to the negative effect on unemployment, an increase in w will also create a negative externality on the policy-maker by raising CPI inflation. As a result, the union's incentive to set a high nominal wage rate is stronger at the non-cooperative equilibrium. Next consider money-supply settings under the two regimes. From equations (14) and (16) it is apparent that the money stock is larger at the non-cooperative equilibrium than at the cooperative equilibrium. The reason for this lies in the impact of a monetary expansion on CPI. For any given nominal wage, a monetary expansion will increase employment but will also have an adverse effect on CPI by causing increases in both domestic good prices and import prices through the real exchange rate. The increase in CPI will affect both the policy-maker's objective and the union's objective through its negative influence on the real consumer wage. At the non-cooperative equilibrium, the policy-maker does not take ínto account the impact of his actions on the union's objectives. Therefore, he will choose a relatively more expansionary monetary policy. When, on the other hand, the policy-maker and the union cooperate, the policy-maker will take explicitly into account the adverse impact of a rise in m on real consumption wages and thus he will be prepared to choose a lower money stock.

Having found wage settings and money supply settings, one may combine equations (14), (16) and (10) to obtain the equilibrium values of n, q and w_c.

We shall focus first on a situation of no migration. When the two players are playing Nash against one another, the equilibrium values of employment, CPI and real consumer wage are:

$$n^N_{NM} = \ell_0 - (bd/2s)$$

$$q^N_{NM} = (b/2c)$$

$$(w_c)^N_{NM} = - (d/s)\, \ell_0 + (bd^2/2s^2) \tag{17a}$$

When they cooperate, the equilibrium values of n, q and w_c are:

$$n^C_{NM} = \ell_0 - (bd/4s)$$

$$q^C_{NM} = 0$$

$$(w_c)^C_{NM} = - (d/s)\, \ell_0 + (bd^2/4s^2) \tag{17b}$$

The relatively higher nominal wage rate at the non-cooperative equilibrium leads to lower employment than under cooperation. The relatively higher nominal wage rate and the relatively larger money supply at the non-cooperative equilibrium also leads to a non-zero CPI inflation. Finally, the relatively higher nominal wage rate at the non-cooperative equilibrium, on balance, leads to a higher real consumer wage than under cooperation. From (17a) and (17b) it is straightforward to establish how each regime affects the position of the two players:

$$U^N_{NM} = - (bd/s)\, \ell_0 + (b^2d^2/4s^2) \tag{18a.1}$$

$$V^N_{NM} = - b^2\delta_2/4cs^2 \tag{18a.2}$$

$$U^C_{NM} = - (bd/s)\, \ell_0 + (0.1875\, b^2d^2/s^2) \tag{18b.1}$$

$$V^C_{NM} = - (0.0625\, b^2d^2/s^2) \tag{18b.2}$$

where $\delta_2 = s^2 + cd^2$.

From (18a) and (18b) it is apparent that:

$$U^N_{NM} > U^C_{NM}, \quad V^N_{NM} < V^C_{NM}$$

That is, the union's welfare is higher at the non-cooperative equilibrium. At the same time, the lower unemployment rate and the zero CPI inflation rate under the cooperative regime implies that the policy-maker is better off under this regime than under the non-cooperative one.

In the context of our model, the size of migration outflows, and thus the size of the effective labour force, is affected by the actions of the two players simply because the wage differential between the home economy and the rest of the world depends on the domestic nominal wage rate and the money supply. Indeed, at the time they make decisions, the two players know that their actions will affect the level of the effective labour force. For example, the choice of a relatively high nominal wage will, other things being equal, lead to a larger effective labour force. Also, the choice of a relative expansionary monetary policy, through the impact of the real exchange rate depreciation on the real consumption wages, will lead to larger migration outflows and thus to a smaller effective labour force. These changes in the level of the effective labour force will affect unemployment levels and thus the utility of the two players. The presence, therefore, of international migration gives rise to two issues. First, does international migration affect the ranking of the cooperative and non-cooperative regimes from the point of view of one of the players or both players? Second, does international migration affect the players' absolute level of utility under the two regimes relative to the case of no migration?

Let us first focus on the first issue. Combining equations (14), (16) and (10) we obtain equilibrium values of n, n_0, q and w_c under international migration. When the two players are playing Nash against one another these values are:

$$n^N_M = (s/\kappa) \, \ell_0 - (bds/2\kappa^2) - (\sigma s/\kappa)(w_c{}^* - \mu)$$

$$(n_0)^N_M = (s/\kappa) \, \ell_0 + \{\sigma bd \, [d + v(1 - h)]/2\kappa^2\} - (\sigma s/\kappa)(w_c{}^* - \mu)$$

$$q^N_M = (0.5b/c)$$

$$(w_c)^N_M = - (d/\kappa)\ell_0 + (bd^2/2\kappa^2) + (\sigma d/\kappa)(w_c{}^* - \mu) \qquad (19a)$$

When the two players cooperate, the equilibrium values of n, n_0, q and w_c are:

$$n^C_M = (s/\kappa) \, \ell_0 - (bds/4\kappa^2) - (\sigma s/\kappa)(w_c{}^* - \mu)$$

$$(n_0)^C_M = (s/\kappa) \, \ell_0 + \{\sigma bd \, [d + v(1 - h)]/4\kappa^2\} - (\sigma s/\kappa)(w_c{}^* - \mu)$$

$$q^C_M = 0$$

$$(w_c)^C_M = - (d/\kappa) \, \ell_0 + (bd^2/4\kappa^2) + (\sigma d/\kappa)(w_c{}^* - \mu) \qquad (19b)$$

Comparing (14a,b) with (15a,b) and (19a) with (19b), we have that

$$w^N_M > w^C_M$$

$$m^N_M > m^C_M$$

$$n^N_M < n^C_M$$

$$(n_o)^N_M > (n_o)^C_M$$

$$q^N_{NM} = q^N_M > q^C_M = q^C_{NM}$$

$$(w_c)^N_M > (w_c)^C_M \tag{20}$$

That is, except for the size of the effective labour force n_o, our findings do not differ from those in the no-migration case, suggesting that international migration does not affect the ranking of the two regimes. Indeed, using (19a) and (19b), it is straightforward to establish the position of the two players under international migration:

$$U^N_M = - (bd/\kappa) \ell_0 + (0.25 \, b^2d^2/\kappa^2) + (\sigma bd/\kappa) (w_c{}^* - \mu)$$

$$V^N_M = - 0.25 \, b^2 \, \delta_1/c\kappa^2 \tag{21a}$$

and

$$U^C_M = - (\frac{bd}{\kappa}) \ell_0 + (0.1875 \, b^2d^2/\kappa^2) + (\sigma bd/\kappa) (w_c{}^* - \mu)$$

$$V^C_M = - (0.0625 \, b^2d^2/\kappa^2) \tag{21b}$$

where $\delta_1 = \kappa^2 + cd^2$.

From (21a) and (21b) it is apparent that:

$$U^N_M > U^C_M \, , \, V^N_M < V^C_M \tag{22}$$

Let us now focus on the second issue, namely whether the presence of international migration affects the absolute level of the players' utility. From (18a,b) and (21a,b) we have:

$$u^N_{NM} > u^N_M > u^C_M < u^C_{NM}$$

$$q^N_{NM} = q^N_M = (b/2c) > q^C_M = q^C_{NM} = 0$$

$$V^N_{NM} < V^N_M < V^C_M > V^C_{NM} \text{ and } U^N_M > U^C_M \tag{23}$$

where $u = n_o - n$ is the unemployment rate. With smaller unemployment due to international migration and with no effect of international migration on CPI, the position of the policy-maker is improved under migration in both regimes. As far as the union is concerned, the presence of international migration affects its welfare through two channels. First, by reducing the effective labour force and thus lowering the domestic unemployment, international migration contributes a positive effect on the union's utility. This effect will be stronger the larger is the initial level of unemployment and thus the larger is ℓ_0. Second, the presence of international migration will deter the union from setting high nominal wages since this will lead to a larger labour force through migration flows. This has a negative effect on union's utility. The second effect will be weaker the higher is the foreign wage rate: high foreign wages will allow the home union to set relatively high domestic wages without running the risk of causing a rise in the effective labour force through migration flows. If the positive effect dominates, then the presence of international migration will on balance increase the union's welfare. The condition for this to be the case is

$$\varphi \ell_0 - \left[\frac{bd(s + \kappa)\,\varphi}{4\kappa s} - s(w_c{}^* - \mu) \right] > 0 \tag{24}$$

where $\varphi = d + v(1 - h)$.

If (24) holds, then the presence of international migration will improve the position of the both players in each regime and thus it will consist a Pareto improvement relative to the no migration situation.

3   International Migration in a Two-Country Model and Games Between Unions and Policy-Makers

In this section we extend the model analysed in section 2 to a two-country setting. The model is summarised by equations (1)–(18), where unstarred (starred) variables refer to the home (foreign) economy.[5]

$$y = v_0 + vn, \qquad\qquad 0 < v_0,\ v < 1 \tag{1}$$

$$y^* = v_0 + vn^* \tag{2}$$

$$n = -(1-v)^{-1}(w-p) + \pi_0, \qquad \pi_0 = (1-v)^{-1} \tag{3}$$

$$n^* = -(1-v)^{-1} (w^* - p^*) + \pi_0 \tag{4}$$

$$y - y^* = sz \tag{5}$$

$$z \equiv e + p^* - p \tag{6}$$

$$q \equiv p + hz \tag{7}$$

$$q^* \equiv p - hz \tag{8}$$

$$w_c = w - q \tag{9}$$

$$w_c^* = w^* - q^* \tag{10}$$

$$m = p + y \tag{11}$$

$$m^* = p^* + y^* \tag{12}$$

$$V = -(n-n_0)^2 - cq^2, \qquad c > 0 \tag{13}$$

$$V^* = -(n^* - n_0^*)^2 - cq^2 \tag{14}$$

$$U = -(n-n_0)^2 + bw_c, \qquad b > 0 \tag{15}$$

$$U^* = -(n^* - n_0^*)^2 + bw_c^* \tag{16}$$

$$n_0 = \ell_0 - \sigma(w_c^* - w_c), \qquad \sigma > 0 \tag{17}$$

$$n_0^* = \ell_0 + \sigma(w_c^* - w_c) \tag{18}$$

The model of equations (1)–(12) can be solved for y, y*, n, n*, q, q*, w_c, w_c^*, z, p and p* as functions of m, m*, w and w*:

$$y = v(m-w)$$

$$y^* = v(m^* - w^*)$$

$$n = m - w$$

$$n^* = m^* - w^*$$

$$w_c = (1-v)(w-m) - \theta(m - w - m^* + w^*), \quad \theta \equiv hv/s > 0$$

$$w_c^* = (1-v)(w^* - m^*) + \theta(m - w - m^* + w^*)$$

$$z = \frac{v}{s} (m - w - m^* + w^*)$$

$$q = (1-v)m + vw + \theta(m - w - m^* + w^*)$$

$$q^* = (1-v)m^* + vw^* - \theta(m - w - m^* + w^*)$$

$$p = vw + (1-v)m$$

$$p^* = vw^* + (1-v)m^* \tag{19}$$

As far as each country's effective labour force is concerned, we can rewrite (17) and (18) as

$$n_0 = \ell_0 - \sigma\tau(m - w - m^* + w^*), \qquad \tau = 1 - v + 2\theta > 0 \tag{20}$$

$$n_0^* = \ell_0 + \sigma\tau(m - w - m^* + w^*) \tag{21}$$

An increase in the home (foreign) money supply, by lowering the home (foreign) real consumer wage and increasing the foreign (home) real consumer wage through the depreciation (appreciation) of the real exchange rate, will induce migration flows from the home (foreign) country to the foreign (home) country. Accordingly, the effective labour force at home (abroad) will fall while the effective labour force abroad (home) will rise. An increase in the home (foreign) nominal wage will increase the home (foreign) real consumer wage. It will also reduce the foreign (home) real consumer wage through the real exchange-rate appreciation (depreciation). Thus it will induce migration flows towards the home (foreign) economy which will in turn result in an increase in the home (foreign) labour force.

The two unions are assumed not to cooperate between themselves or with the policy-makers. In a non-cooperative environment, then, the home union, having formed expectations about money supplies will set w so as to maximise (15) treating w* as given, i.e. it will solve

$$\max_{w} U \text{ s.t.(19) and } \frac{\partial w^*}{\partial w} = 0$$

This leads to the Nash reaction function (22):

$$w = -\frac{\ell_0}{\sigma_1} + m - \frac{\sigma\tau}{\sigma_1}(m^* - w^*) + \frac{b\tau_1}{2\sigma_1^2} \qquad (22)$$

where $\tau = 1 - v + 2\theta > 0$, $\qquad \tau_1 = 1 - v + \theta > 0$, $\qquad \sigma_1 = 1 + \sigma\tau > 0$.

The foreign union's reaction function, describing its best play for different moves by the home union, can be found in a similar way:

$$w^* = -\frac{\ell_0}{\sigma_1} + m^* - \frac{\sigma\tau}{\sigma_1}(m - w) + \frac{b\tau_1}{2\sigma_1^2} \qquad (23)$$

In the home (foreign) union's reaction function, the home (foreign) nominal wage w (w^*) and the initial labour force ℓ_0 are negatively related: a large initial labour force will require the home (foreign) union to set a low nominal wage in order to keep unemployment low. The home (foreign) nominal wage w (w^*) and the money supply m (m^*) are positively related: other things being equal, an increase in m (m^*), by increasing domestic (foreign) employment and reducing the home (foreign) effective labour force, will result in lower home (foreign) unemployment; the increase in m (m^*) will also lower real consumer wages through its impact on CPI inflation. Therefore, the home (foreign) union will react by increasing w (w^*), by an equal amount so as to preserve an unchanged (home) real consumer wage and an unchanged level of unemployment. An increase in the foreign (home) money supply, by causing a real exchange rate appreciation, will create a real-wage-differential in favour of the home (foreign) country and thus will induce migration flows into the home (foreign) economy. This will result in an increase in the home (foreign) effective labour force and thus in home (foreign) unemployment. Therefore, the home (foreign) union will react by lowering its nominal wage so as to offset the adverse impact of the increase in m^*(m) on unemployment. On the other hand, an increase in w^* (w) will leave the home (foreign) economy with a smaller effective-labour force, and thus with less unemployment. This will allow the home (foreign) union to set a relatively higher nominal wage rate.

Solving the two reaction functions for w and w^* we obtain:

$$w = -\ell_0 + m + \frac{b\tau_1}{2\sigma_1} \tag{24}$$

$$w^* = -\ell_0 + m^* + \frac{b\tau_1}{2\sigma_1} \tag{25}$$

As far as money-supply setting is concerned, we consider two regimes: home and foreign policy-makers may behave as non-cooperative players, each treating the other's money-supply setting as given when choosing monetary policy, or they may cooperate in which case each will set monetary policy so that his marginal rate of substitution between m and m* equals unity. Starting with the non-cooperative regime, the home policy-maker will maximise (13) treating m* as parametric:

$$\max_{m} V \text{ s.t (19) and } \frac{\partial m^*}{\partial m} = 0$$

This leads to the reaction function (26):

$$m = \frac{\sigma_1}{c\tau_1^2 + \sigma_1^2}\ell_0 + \frac{c\tau_1^2(\theta\text{-v}) + \sigma_1^2}{c\tau_1^2 + \sigma_1^2}w + \frac{\sigma_2}{c\tau_1^2 + \sigma_1^2}(m^* - w^*) \tag{26}$$

where $\sigma_2 = c\theta\tau_1 + \sigma\sigma_1\tau > 0$, $v - \theta > 0$.

Similarly, the foreign policy-maker's reaction function is

$$m^* = \frac{\sigma_1}{c\tau_1^2 + \sigma_1^2}\ell_0 + \frac{c\tau_1^2(\theta\text{-v}) + \sigma_1^2}{c\tau_1^2 + \sigma_1^2}w^* + \frac{\sigma_2}{c\tau_1^2 + \sigma_1^2}(m - w) \tag{27}$$

A large initial home (foreign) labour force will require a relatively expansionary monetary policy at home (abroad) to keep unemployment low. Therefore, in (26)–(27), money supplies and the initial labour force ℓ_0 are positively related. On the other hand, a rise in w (w*) will have two opposing effects on m (m*). First, it will lead to a rise in home (foreign) CPI, thus requiring a fall in the home (foreign) money supply to keep q (q*) unchanged. Second, the rise in w (w*), will reduce employment demand and by inducing migration flows into the home (foreign) economy it will also increase the home (foreign) effective labour force and thus home (foreign) unemployment. The second effect will require an expansionary monetary policy at home (abroad) to keep unemployment low. Therefore, the overall effect of a rise in w (w*) on m (m*) is indeterminate.

An increase in the foreign (home) money supply, by causing a real exchange rate appreciation (depreciation), will induce migration flows into home (foreign) country thus resulting in an increase the home (foreign) effective labour force. This will require an increase in m (m*) to keep home (foreign) unemployment unchanged. An increase in the foreign (home) nominal wage, by inducing flows of labour away from the home (foreign) economy, will lower home (foreign) unemployment and will thus require a smaller money stock.

Making use of the fact that due to the symmetry of the model the two unions will choose the same nominal wage, we find the following non-cooperative money-supply settings:[6]

$$m^N = \frac{\sigma_1}{c\tau_1\,(1\text{-}v) + \sigma_1}\,\ell_0 - \frac{(c\tau_1\,v - \sigma_1)}{c\tau_1\,(1\text{-}v) + \sigma_1}\,w \qquad (28)$$

$$m^{*N} = \frac{\sigma_1}{c\tau_1\,(1\text{-}v) + \sigma_1}\,\ell_0 - \frac{(c\tau_1\,v - \sigma_1)}{c\tau_1\,(1\text{-}v) + \sigma_1}\,w^* \qquad (29)$$

Consider next the cooperative regime. Following, e.g. Canzoneri and Henderson (1988), Rogoff (1985), Jensen (1993a,b) and Zervoyianni (1993), we assume that the two policy-makers will choose m and m* with a view to maximising the sum of their objective functions:

$$\max_{m,m^*} V + V^* \text{ s.t (20) and } \frac{\partial m^*}{\partial m} = 0, \frac{\partial m}{\partial m^*} = 0$$

This leads to the following cooperative money-supply settings:[7]

$$m^C = \frac{1}{1 + c(1\text{-}v)^2}\,\ell_0 + \frac{1 - cv\,(1\text{-}v)}{1 + c(1\text{-}v)^2}\,w \qquad (30)$$

$$m^{*C} = \frac{1}{1 + c(1\text{-}v)^2}\,\ell_0 + \frac{1 - cv\,(1\text{-}v)}{1 + c(1\text{-}v)^2}\,w^* \qquad (31)$$

Let us compare money-supply settings in the two regimes. Subtracting (30) from (28) and simplifying we have:

$$m^N - m^C = \frac{c\alpha_2}{\alpha_1} \ [(1-v)\ell_0 + w] \tag{32}$$

where $\alpha_1 = [1 + c(1-v)^2] \ [(1-v)c\tau_1 + \sigma_1] > 0$
$\alpha_2 = -\theta + (1-v) \ \sigma\tau \lessgtr 0$

Clearly, whether money supply will be larger under a Nash regime than under a cooperative regime will depend on the sign of the expression α_2. In a situation of no international migration, $\sigma = 0$, $\sigma_1 = 1$ and $\alpha_2 = -\theta$ and so it follows that $m^N < m^C$. In other words, monetary policy in each country will be more expansionary when the policy-makers cooperate than when they do not cooperate. This is the Rogoff's (1985) result. Indeed, quoting Zervoyianni (1993):

> ... This is because, given the actions of the unions, each policy-maker knows that any unilateral monetary expansion will have an adverse effect on his country's CPI both because it will increase domestic-good prices and because it will increase import prices by depreciating the exchange rate. The impact on CPI inflation of the exchange-rate response to any unilateral monetary expansion reduces the incentives of each policy-maker to make an effort to influence domestic employment. When, however, the policy-makers cooperate, each knows that the negative influence of a domestic monetary expansion on his country's CPI via the exchange rate will be offset by an equal expansion abroad. Thus both have a relatively stronger incentive to take actions aimed at raising domestic employment to the level of the effective labour force. Given the actions of the unions, this leads them to choose more expansionary monetary policies at the cooperative equilibrium than at the non-cooperative equilibrium ...

In the presence of international migration, however, in addition to increasing employment at the expense of higher CPI inflation, a unilateral monetary expansion will also induce migration flows and this will affect the size of the effective labour force in both countries. Thus with $\sigma > 0$, each policy-maker perceives that any unilateral monetary expansion will result in lower unemployment by both increasing his country's employment and decreasing his country's effective labour force. In other words, the presence of international migration allows each policy-maker to exercise an additional positive influence on unemployment in his country by increasing the money supply.

How will policy-makers use this additional influence on unemployment? Will a non-cooperative policy-maker choose a more expansionary policy under conditions of international migration than without international migration?

Comparing the Nash money supplies in the absence of international migration with those under migration we have:

$$m^N{}_{NM} < m^N{}_M \text{ and } m^{*N}{}_{NM} < m^{*N}{}_M$$

That is, in a non-cooperative regime money supplies will be more expansionary under conditions of international migration than under conditions of no international migration.

As far as the cooperative regime is concerned, it is apparent from (30) and (31) that, given w and w*, international migration does not affect money-supply settings. The reason behind this result is that under cooperation, each policy-maker takes into account that the influence of a domestic monetary expansion on his country's unemployment via the induced reduction in the effective labour force will be offset by an equal expansion abroad. Thus both policy makers realise that they have no power to affect their country's unemployment through the effective labour force and therefore neither of them will be willing to use monetary policy in order to induce migration flows. This effectively implies that in the case of cooperation macroeconomic interdependence through migration flows becomes inoperative.

Combining equations (24), (25), (28) and (29) we obtain the following equilibrium values for nominal wages and money stocks when all players are playing Nash against one another:

$$w^N = -(1\text{-}v)\,\ell_0 + \frac{b[c\tau_1\,(1\text{-}v) + 1 + \sigma\tau]}{2c\,(1 + \sigma\tau)}$$

$$m^N = v\ell_0 - \frac{b[c\tau_1 v - \sigma\tau - 1]}{2c\,(1 + \sigma\tau)} \tag{33}$$

Similarly, combining equations (24), (25), (30) and (31), we obtain equilibrium values for nominal wages and money supplies when the unions behave as Nash players while the policy-makers cooperate with each other and play Nash jointly against the unions:

$$w^C = -(1\text{-}v)\,\ell_0 + \frac{b\tau_1\,[(1 + c(1\text{-}v)^2]}{2c\,(1\text{-}v)\,(1 + \sigma\tau)}$$

$$m^C = v\ell_0 + \frac{b\tau_1 \left[(1 - (1-v) \, cv\right]}{2c \ (1+\sigma\tau)(1-v)} \tag{34}$$

Comparison of the equilibrium money-supply settings and nominal-wage settings under the two regimes reveals that:

$$m^C \gtreqless m^N \text{ and } w^C \gtreqless w^N \text{ if } \alpha_2 = -\theta + (1-v) \, \sigma\tau \lesseqgtr 0 \tag{35}$$

The expression α_2 captures two effects. First is the negative influence of unilateral monetary expansions on CPIs via the real exchange rate. This is reflected in the first term, i.e. $-\theta$. Second is the positive influence of unilateral monetary expansions on unemployment via international migration. Under a cooperative regime both effects are internalised. Under a non-cooperative regime each policy-maker will have to bear the inflation costs of exchange-rate changes associated with monetary expansions aimed at increasing employment but he will be in a position to influence his country's unemployment through international migration. Therefore, if the (expected) positive effect on unemployment through international migration, is stronger than the negative effect on the CPI via the real exchange rate, i.e. $\alpha_2 > 0$, each policy-maker will choose a more expansionary monetary policy in the non-cooperative regime than in the cooperative regime. In this case, the more expansionary policy in the non-cooperative regime will create a relatively higher CPI inflation rate than in the cooperative regime and each trade union will set higher nominal wages to keep unchanged real consumption wages.

Having found wage settings and money supply settings under both regimes we can now combine them with (19) to obtain the equilibrium levels of employment, effective labour force, real consumer wages and CPIs:

$$n^N = n^C = \ell_0 - \frac{b\tau_1}{2(1+\sigma\tau)}$$

$$w_c^N = w_c^C = -(1-v) \, \ell_0 + \frac{b(1-v)\tau_1}{2(1+\sigma\tau)}$$

$$n_0 = n_0{}^* = \ell_0$$

$$q^N = \frac{b}{2c} \quad , q^C = \frac{b\tau_1}{2 \ (1-v) \ c(1+\sigma\tau)} \tag{36}$$

From (37) it follows that

$$q^N > q^C \qquad \text{if } \alpha_2 = -\theta + (1-v) \, \sigma\tau > 0 \tag{36a}$$

That is, a more expansionary monetary policy in the non-cooperative regime, i.e. $\alpha_2 > 0$, will result in a relative higher CPI inflation rate.

From (13)–(16) it is straightforward to establish how each regime affects the positions of the unions and policy-makers:

$$U^N = U^C = U*^N = U*^C = - (1-v)b\ell_0 - \frac{b\tau^2_1[\tau_1 - 2(1-v)\,\sigma_1]}{4\sigma_1^2}$$

$$V^N = V*^N = - \frac{b^2[c\tau_1^2 + \sigma_1^2]}{4c\sigma_1^2}$$

$$V^C = V*^C = - \frac{b^2\tau_1^2[1 + c(1-v)^2]}{4c\sigma_1^2(1-v)^2} \tag{37}$$

As far as the unions are concerned their welfare is the same in both regimes: as is evident from (36), real consumption wages and unemployment levels do not differ across regimes. However, as far as the policy-makers are concerned, their positions depends critically on CPI inflation which differs between the two regimes, i.e. (36a). Indeed from (37) we obtain the result:

$$V^N < V^C \qquad \text{if } \alpha_2 = -\theta + (1-v)\,\sigma\tau > 0$$

Assuming, for example, that $v = (1-v) = \frac{1}{2}$, and taking into account the definition of θ and τ, the condition for α_2 to be positive becomes

$$\alpha_2 = - \frac{2h}{s}\,(1-\sigma) + \sigma > 0 \tag{38}$$

This condition is satisfied if the sensitivity of migration flows to changes in real wage differentials is sufficiently strong, e.g. if one-unit increase in the real-wage differential (w_c*-w_c) results in a one-unit migration flows between the two countries. Even if σ is less than unity, however, condition (38) is most likely to be satisfied since $h < \frac{1}{2}$ and $s > 1$.

The explanation why condition (38) needs to be satisfied if V^N is to be smaller than V^C lies in the strength of externalities between countries arising from the effect of real-exchange-rate changes on national CPIs relative to those arising from migration flows. As we have already explained, the first term in (38) reflects the externalities arising from real-exchange-rate effects on CPIs while the second term reflects international macroeconomic interdependence arising from labour flows between countries. If the impact on national welfare levels of the externality arising from international labour flows is stronger than that arising from the effect of real-exchange-rate changes on CPIs, then the second term in (38) will be the largest of the two and cooperation between home and foreign policy-makers will lead to a Pareto improvement relative to the Nash regime. This result contrasts with the findings of e.g. Jensen (1993a, b) and Rogoff (1985) that monetary cooperation between policy-makers is always counterproductive: with international labour mobility, inter-government cooperation in the monetary field may well turn out to be advantageous.

4   Conclusions

In this chapter we have incorporated the possibility of international migration into a monetary policy game played by governments and trade unions in open economies. In the small-open-economy context, international migration is found not to affect the ranking of the cooperative and non-cooperative regimes from the point of view of each player. However, it improves the absolute position of each player under both regimes and thus it constitutes a Pareto-improvement relative to the no migration situation. This is because international migration affects the size of the effective labour force and has no effect on CPI inflation: this creates a positive externality for both players which improves their absolute positions. In a two-country context we show that contrary to usual presumptions, established by earlier studies that ignore the possibility of international migration, inter-government cooperation in the monetary field may well turn out to be advantageous.

Notes

1   For macroeconomic policy games in the closed economy see e.g. Barro and Gordon (1983), Calmfors and Horn (1985), Driffill (1984, 1986), Hersoug (1986) and Calmfors and Driffill (1988).

2   To focus on international migration we assume no capital mobility. A more realist model would allow for international mobility of capital as well as labour. This is left for future research.

3   Note that the foreign real consumption wage in home currency purchasing-power units, W_c^f, can be expressed as

$$W^f_c = \frac{W^*_c\, P^*_c\, E}{P_c}$$

where

W^*_c is the foreign real consumer wage in foreign-currency purchasing power units

P^*_c is the foreign real consumer prices in foreign -currency purchasing power units

$P_c \equiv P^{(1-h)}(EP^*)^h = PZ^h$ is the home country's CPI

E is the nominal exchange rate (defined as the home currency price of foreign currency)

$Z \equiv \dfrac{EP^*}{P}$ is the real exchange rate.

Using the definition of P_c and normalising P_c^* and P^* to unity we have

$W^f_c = W^*_c\, Z^{(1-h)}$ which, in logs, reads as in the main text.

4   Equation (7) is based on the assumption of no capital mobility and no interest-bearing assets. In particular, following e.g. Zervoyianni (1993), we assume that an increase in the real exchange rate by improving the home country's competitiveness will lead to a trade balance surplus while an increase in domestic output relative to foreign output will lead to a trade balance deficit:

$$TB = S_1 z - S_2(y-y^*)$$

Assuming no capital mobility, trade must be balanced. Thus $TB = 0$ and the equilibrium real exchange rate is:

$$z = S_2/S_1\ (y-y^*)$$

Normalising y^* to zero and solving for y in terms of z we obtain

$y = sz$, where $s = \dfrac{S_1}{S_2}$

Empirical evidence suggests that for most countries changes in the real exchange rate have a stronger effect on the trade balance than changes in income through (net) import demand, i.e. $S_1 > S_2$, that allows us to obtain $s > 1$.

5   Where in (17)–(18) we have omitted, for simplicity, migration costs. Note also that in the context of our model the world (effective) labour force is constant, i.e.

$$n_0 + n_0^* = \ell_0 + \ell_0 = 2\ell_0$$

6   This is just to simplify the expressions for m and m^* in (27) and (28) and it does not affect our results as far as equilibrium employment, CPIs and real consumer wages are concerned.

7   As in the previous footnote this is just to simplify our expressions for m and m*. In principle, however, the full expressions for m and m* are

$$m = \frac{\alpha_{11}}{\kappa} \cdot w + \frac{2\sigma_2}{\kappa} \quad m^* - \frac{\alpha_{22}}{\kappa} \quad w^* + \frac{\ell_0}{\kappa}$$

$$m^* = \frac{\alpha_{11}}{\kappa} \quad w^* + \frac{2\sigma_2}{\kappa} \quad m - \frac{\alpha_{22}}{\kappa} \quad w + \frac{\ell_0}{\kappa}$$

where

$$\alpha_{11} = c(\tau\theta - \tau_1 v) + 2\sigma^2\,\tau^2 + 2\sigma\tau + 1$$

$$\alpha_{22} = c\theta(\tau_1 + \theta - v) + 2\sigma\,\sigma_1\tau$$

$$\sigma_2 = c\tau_1\theta + \sigma\,\sigma_1\tau$$

Using the above expressions yields the same solutions for n, n*, q , q*, w_c and w_c^* as those in (30) and (31).

References

Abbott, M. and Ashenfelter, O. (1976), 'Labour Supply, Commodity Demand and the Allocation of Time', *Review of Economic Studies*, 43, pp. 389–411.

Abowd, J.M. and Freeman, R.B. (1991), *Immigration, Trade, and the Labour Market*, Chicago: The University of Chicago Press.

Ahtiala, P. (1989), 'A Note on Fiscal Policy Under Flexible Exchange Rates', *European Economic Review*, 33, pp. 1481–86.

Akerlof, G., Rose, A. and Yallen, J. (1988), 'Job Switching and Job Satisfaction in the US Labour market', *Brooking Papers of Economic Activity*, 2, pp. 530–56.

Allen, P.A. and Kennen, P.B. (1980), *Asset Markets, Exchange Rates and Economic Integration: A synthesis*, Cambridge: Cambridge University Press.

Alogoskoufis, G. (1994), 'On Inflation, Unemployment, and the Optimal Exchange Rate Regime' in Ploeg, V.D. (ed.), *Handbook of International Macroeconomics*, pp. 192–223, Oxford: Blackwell.

Alogoskoufis, G. and Manning, A. (1988), 'On the Persistence of Unemployment', *Economic Policy*, 3, pp. 427–69.

Aoki, M. (1981), *Dynamic Analysis of Open Economies*, New York: Academic Press.

Argy, V. and Salop, J. (1983), 'Price and Output Effects of Monetary Expansion in a Two-country World Under Flexible Exchange Rates', *Oxford Economic Papers*, 35, pp. 228–46.

Baldwin, R. and Venables, A. (1994), 'International Migration, Capital Mobility and Transitional Dynamics', *Economica*, 61, pp. 285–300.

Barro, R.J. and Gordon, D.B. (1983), 'A positive Theory of Monetary Policy in a National Rate Model', *Journal of Political Economy*, 91, pp. 589–610.

Barzel, Y. and McDonald, R. (1973), 'Assets, Subsistence and the Supply Curve of Labour', *American Economic Review*, 63, pp. 621–32.

Bhagwati, J. and Hamada, K. (1974), 'Brain Drain, International Integration and Markets for Professional and Unemployment: A Theoretical Analysis', *Journal of Development Economics*, 1, pp. 19–42.

Bhagwati, J. and Rodriguez, C. (1983), 'Welfare – Theoretical Analysis of the Brain Drain' in Bhagwati, J. (ed.), *Essays in International Economic Theory*, Vol. 2, pp. 75–102, Cambridge, Massachusetts: MIT Press.

Bhandari, J. and Genberg, H. (1989), 'Exchange Rate Movements and International Interdependence of Stock Markets', *IMF Working Paper*, No. 44, Washington DC, May.

Blanchard, O. and Fischer, S. (1989), *Lectures on Macroeconomics*, Cambridge, Massachusetts: MIT Press.

Blanchard, O. and Summers, L. (1986), 'Hysteresis and the European Unemployment Problem', *N.B.E.R. Macroeconomic Annual*, Cambridge, Mass.: M.I.T. Press.

Booth, A. and Chatterji, M. (1993), 'Union Membership and Wage Bargaining when Membership is not Compulsory', University of Dundee Discussion Paper, July 1993.

Borjas, G. (1991), *Friends or Strangers: the Impact of Immigration on the U.S. Economy*, New York: Basic Books.

Borjas, G. and Freeman, R. (1992), *Immigration and the Workforce: Economic Consequences for the United States and Source Areas*, Chicago: NBER, University of Chicago Press.

Brecher, R. and Choudhri, E. (1987), 'International Migration Versus Foreign Investment in the Presence of Unemployment', *Journal of International Economics*, 23, pp. 329–42.

Brecher, R. and Choudhri, E. (1990), 'Gains from International Factor Movements without Lump-Sum Compensation: Taxation by Location Versus Nationality', *Canadian Journal of Economics*, 23, pp. 44–59.

Burda, M. (1993), 'The Determinants of East-West German Migration', *European Economic Review*, 37, pp. 425–61.

Burda, M. and Wyplosz, C. (1992), 'Human Capital, Investment, and Migration in an Integrated Europe', *European Economic Review*, 36, pp. 667–84.

Burmeister, E. and Dowell, A.R. (1970), *Mathematical Theories of Economic Growth*, London: Collier-McMillan.

Burmeister, E . (1980), *Capital Theory and Dynamics*, Cambridge: Cambridge University Press.

Calmfors, L. and Driffill, E.J. (1988), 'Bargaining Structure, Corporatism and Macroeconomic Performance', *Economic Policy*, 6, pp. 12–61.

Calmfors, L. and Horn, H. (1985), 'Classical Unemployment, Accomodation Policies and the Adjustment of Real Wages', *Scandinavian Journal of Economics*, 87, pp. 92–119.

Canzoneri, M.D. and Henderson D.W. (1988), 'Is Sovereign Policy-making Bad?' in Brunner, K. and Meltzer, A.H. (eds), *Stabilisation Policies and Labour Markets*, Garnegie-Rochester Conference Series on Public Policy, No. 28, Spring.

Carlin, W. and Soskice, D. (1990), *Macroeconomics and the Wage Bargain*, Oxford: Oxford University Press.

Carruth, A. and Oswald, A. (1987), 'On Union Preferences and Labour Market Models: Insiders and Outsiders', *Economic Journal*, 97, pp. 431–45.

Chen, Chau-Nau (1975), 'Economic Growth, Portfolio Balance, and the Balance of Payments', *Canadian Journal of Economics*, 88, pp. 24–33.

Chesnais, J.C. (1992), 'Recent Migratory Movements' in Salt, J. (ed.), *People on the Move, New Migration Flows in Europe*, Council of Europe, Council of Europe Press, pp. 11–40.

Creedy, J. and McDonald, I. (1991), 'Models of Trade Union Behaviour: A Synthesis', *Economic Record*, 61, pp. 346–59.

Clarke, H.R. and Ng, Y. (1993), 'Immigration and Economic Welfare', *The Economic Record*, 69, No. 206, pp. 259.

Cubitt, R.P. (1992), 'Monetary Policy Games and Private Sector Precommitment', *Oxford Economic Papers*, 44, pp. 513–30.

De New, J.P. and Zimmerman, K.F. (1993a), 'Blue Color Vulnerability: Wage Impacts of Migration' in Steinmann, G. and Ulrich, R. (eds), *Economic Consequences of Immigration to Germany*, Berlin: Springer-Verlag.

De New, J.P. and Zimmerman, K.F. (1993b), 'Native Wage Impacts of Foreign Labor: A Random Effect Panel analysis', *Journal of Population Economics*.

Devereux, M. and Purvis, D. (1990), 'Fiscal Policy and the Real Excgange Rate', *European Economic Review*, 34, pp. 1201–11.

Djajic, S. (1985), 'Minimum Wage, Unemployment and International Migration', mimeograph, Queen's University Discussion Paper, February.

Djajic, S. (1987), 'Illegal Aliens, Unemployment And Immigration Policy', *Journal of Development Economics*, 25, pp. 235–49.

Djajic, S. (1989), 'Migrants, in a Guest-Worker System: A Utility Maximizing Approach, *Journal of Development Economics*, 31, pp. 327–39.

Dolado, J, Alessandra, G. and Ichino, A. (1993), 'Immigration; Human capital and Growth in the Host Country', paper presented at the Coneference on *The Economics of International Migration*, organized by the University of Konstanz, 26–27 February.

Drazen, A and Gottfries, N. (1990), 'The Persistence of Unemployment in a Dynamic Insider-Outsider Model' in Weiss, Y. and Fischelson, G. (eds), *Advances in the Theory and Measurement of Employment*, pp. 323–35.

Driffill, J. (1984), 'Can Stabilization Policy Increase the Equilibrium Unemployment Rate?' in Hutchinson, G. and Treble, J.G. (eds), *Recent Advances in Labour Economics*, London: Croom-Helm.

Driffill, J. (1986), 'Macroeconomic Stabilisation Policy and Trade Union Behavior as a Repeated Game' in Calmfors, L. and Horn, H. (eds), *Trade Unions, Wage Formation and Macroeconomic Stability*, London: Macmillan, pp. 158–84.

Driffill, J. and Schultz, C. (1992), 'Wage Setting and Stabilisation Policy in a Game with Renegotiation', *Oxford Economic Papers*, 44, pp. 440–59.

Driskill, R. and McCafferty, S. (1987), 'Exchange-Rate Determination: An Equilibrium Approach With Imperfect Capital Substitutability', *Journal of International Economics*, 23, pp. 241–61.

Dornbush, R. (1976a), 'Capital mobility, Flexible Exchange Rates and Macroeconomic Equilibrium' in Classen, E. and Salin, P. (eds), *Recent Issues in International Monetary Economics*, Amsterdam: North-Holland.

Dornbush, R. (1976b), 'Expectations and Exchange Rate Dynamics', *Journal of Political Economy*, 84, pp. 1161–76.

Eaton, J. and Turnovsky, S. (1983), 'Covered Interest Parity, Uncovered Interest Parity and Exchange Rate Dynamics', *Economic Journal*, 93, pp. 555–75.

Evans, P. and Karras, G. (1993), 'Do Standards of Living Converge?', *Economic Letters*, 43, pp. 149–55.

Faini, R. and Venturini, A. (1993), 'Labour Migration in Europe: Trade, Aid and Migrations', *European Economic Review*, 37, pp. 435–42.

Freeman, R.B. (1978), 'Job Satisfaction as an Economic Variable', *American Economic Review*, 68, pp. 135–41.

Freeman, R.B. (1993), 'Immigration from Poor to Wealthy Countries: Experience of the United States', *European Economic Review*, 37, pp. 443–51.

Frenkel, J. and Rodriguez, C. (1975), 'Portfolio Equilibrium and the Balance of Payments: A Monetary Approach', *American Economic Review*, 63, pp. 674–88.

Ghosh, B. (1992), 'Migratory Movements from Central and East European Countries to Western Europe' in Salt, J. (ed.), *People on the Move: New Migration Flows in Europe*, Council of Europe Press, pp. 143–82.

Gottfries, N. and Horn, H. (1987), 'Wage Formation and the Persistence of Unemployment', *Economic Journal*, 97, pp. 877–86.

Gould, J.P. (1968), 'Adjustment Costs in the Theory of Investment of the Firm', *Review of Economic Studies*, 35, pp. 47–55.

Greenwood, M.J. (1969), 'The Determinants of Labour Migration', *Journal of Regional Science*, 9, No. 2, pp. 283–90.

Greenwood, M.J. and McDowell, J.M. (1986), 'The Factor Market Consequences of U.S. Immigration', *Journal of Economic Literature*, pp. 1738–72.

Gyflanson, T. and Lindbeck, A. (1986), 'Endogenous Unions and Governments: A Game Theoretic Approach', *European Economic Review*, 30, pp. 5–26.

Gyflanson, T. and Lindbeck, A. (1991), *The Interaction of Monetary Policy and Wages*, CEPR Discussion Paper No. 551, July.

Hamermesh, D.S. (1974), 'Enjoyable work and labour supply', unpublished manuscript, Department of Economics, Michigan State University.

Harris, J. and Todaro, M. (1970), 'Migration, Unemployment and Development: A Two-Sector Analysis', *American Economic Review*, 60, pp. 126–42.

Hayes, J. (1971), 'Occupational Perceptions and Occupational Information', Department of Psychology, The University of Leeds.

Hersoug, T. (1986), 'Workers Versus Government: Who Adjusts to Whom?' in Calmfors, L. and Horn, H. (eds), *Trade Unions, Wage Formation and Macroeconomic Stability*, London: Macmillan, pp. 128–50.

Hicks, J.R. (1932), *The Theory of Wages*, London: Macmillan.

Hill, J.K. (1987), 'Immigrant Decisions Concerning Duration of Stay and Migration Frequency', *Journal of Development Economics*, 25, pp. 221–34.

Horn, H. and Persson, T. (1988), 'Exchange Rate Policy, Wage Formation and Credibility', *European Economic Review*, 32, pp. 1621–36.

Ichino, A. (1993), 'The Economic Impact of Immigration on the Host Country' in Luciani, G. (ed.), *Migration Policies in Europe and the United States*, Kluwer Academic Press.

Jensen, H. (1991), 'Tax distortions, Unempolyment and International Policy Cooperation', mimeo, University of Aarhus.

Jensen, H. (1993a), 'Uncertainty in Interdepedent Economies with Monopoy Unions', *Journal of Macroeconomics*, 15, pp. 1–24.

Jensen, H. (1993b), 'International Monetary Policy Cooperation in Economies with centralized Wage Setting', *Open Economies Review*, 4, pp. 269–85.

Johnson, J. and Salt, J. (1990), *Labour Migration*, David Fulton Publishers.

Johnson, P. and Zimmmerman, K. (1992), *Labour Supply in An Ageing Europe*, Cambridge: Cambridge University Press.

Killingsworth, M. (1983), *Labour Supply*, Cambridge: Cambridge University Press.

Kumcu, M.E. (1989), 'The Savings Behaviour of Migrant Workers', *Journal of Development Economics*, 30, pp. 273–86.

Layard, R., Nickell, S. and Jackman, R. (1991), *Unemployment: Macroeconomic Performance and the Labour Market*, Oxford: Oxford University Press.

Layard, R. Nickell, S. and Jackman, R. (1994), *The Unemployment Crisis*, Oxford: Oxford University Press.

Lindbeck, A. (1987), 'Union Activity, Unemployment Persistent and Wage-Employment Ratchets', *European Economic Review Papers and Proceedings*, 31, pp. 157–67.

Lindbeck, A. (1993), *Unemployment and Macroeconomics*, Cambridge, Massachusetts: MIT Press.

Lindbeck, A. and Snower, D. (1986), 'Wage Setting Unemployment and Insider-Outsider Relations', *American Economic Review Papers and Proceedings*, 76, pp. 235–39.

Lucas, R. (1976), 'The Supply of Immigrants' Function and Taxation of Immigrants' Incomes' in Bhagwati, J. (ed.), *The Brain Drain and Taxation*, Amsterdam: North-Holland, pp. 63–82.

McCulloch, R. and Yellen, J. (1975), 'Consequences of a Tax on the Brain Drain for Unemployment and Income Inequality', *Journal of Development Economics*, 2, pp. 249–64.

McDonald, I. and Solow, R. (1981), 'Wage Bargaining and Employment', *American Economic Review*, 71, pp. 891–908.

McKibbin, W.J. and Sachs, J. (1986), 'Coordination of Monetary and Fiscal Policies in the OECD', Cambridge, Massachusetts, National Bureau of Economic Research, Working Paper No. 1800.

Molho, I. (1986), 'Theories of Migration: A Review', *Scottish Journal of Political Economy*, 33, No. 4, pp. 396–419.

Molle, M. and Van Mourik, A. (1988), 'International Movements of Labour under Conditions of Economic Integration: The Case of Western Europe', *Journal of Common Studies*, 26, pp. 317–39.

Mortensen, D. (1970), 'A Theory of Wages and Employment Dynamics' in Phelps, E. (ed.), *Microeconomic Foundations of Employment and Inflation Theory*, New York: W. Norton and Company, pp. 166–211.

Mundell, R.A. (1983), *International Economics*, New York: Macmillan.

Murphy, R. (1989), 'Stock Prices, Real Exchange Rates and Optimal Capital Accumulation', *IMF Staff Papers*, 36, pp. 103–29.

Nickell, S. (1986), 'Dynamic Models of Labour Demand' in Ashenfelter, O. and Layard, R. (eds), *Handbook of Labour Economics*, Vol. 1, pp. 473–99.

Nickell, S. (1990), 'Unemployment: A Survey', *Economic Journal*, 100, pp. 391–439.

Nikas, C. (1992), 'The Causes and The Effects of Migration: A Survey', Discussion Paper No. 131, University of York.

Obstfeld, M. and Stockman, A. (1985), 'Exchange Rate Dynamics' in Jones, R. and Kenen, P. (eds), *Handbook of International Economics*, Vol. 2, Amsterdam: North-Holland.

Okolski, M. (1992), 'Migratory Movements from Countries of Central and Eastern Europe' in Salt, J. (ed.), *People on the Move: New Migration Flows in Europe*, Council of Europe Press, pp. 83–116.

Oswald, A. (1986), 'The Economic Theory of Trade Unions: An Introductory Survey' in Calmfors, L. and Horn, H. (eds), *Trade Unions, Wage Formation and Macroeconomic Stability*, London: Macmillan.

Oudiz, G. and Sachs, J. (1984), 'Macoeconomic Policy Coordination Among The Industrial Economies', *Brooking Papers on Economic Activity*, 1, pp. 1–77.

Parnes, H. and Spitz, R. (1969), 'A Conceptual Framework for Studing Labor Mobility', *Monthly Labor Review*, November.

Pikoulakis, E. (1981), *Foreign Reserves and Balance of Payments Adjustments in a Small Growing Economy under Fixed Exchange Rates*, doctoral dissertation, L.S.E.

Pikoulakis, E. (1984), 'Fiscal and Monetary Policies in a Flexible Exchange Rate Model with Full Employment and Static Expectations' in Black, J. and Dorrance, G. (eds), *Problems of International Finance*, London. Macmillan Press.

Quibria, M. (1989), 'International Migration and Real Wages', *Journal of Developed Economics*, 31, pp. 177–83.

Raffelhuschen, B. (1992), 'Labour Migration in Europe', *European Economic Review*, 36, pp. 1453–71.

Rivera-Batiz, L. (1989), 'The Impact of International Migration on Real Wages', *Journal of Development Economics*, 31, pp. 185–92.

Rodriguez, C. (1976), 'Brain Drain and Economic Growth: A Dynamic Model' in Bhagwati, J. (ed.), *The Brain Drain and Taxation*, Amsterdam: North-Holland, pp. 171–95.

Rogoff, K. (1985), 'Can International Monetary Policy Coordination Be Counterproductive?', *Journal of International Economics*, 18, pp. 199–217.

Russell, S. and Teitelbaum, M. (1992), 'International Migration and International Trade', World Bank Discussion Paper No.160, The World Bank, Washington DC.

Sachs, J. (1980), 'Wages, Flexible Exhange Rates and Macroeconomic policy', *Quarterly Journal of Economics*, 94, pp. 731–47.

Salt, J.C. (1992), 'Current and Future International Migration Trends Affecting Europe' in Salt, J. (ed.), *People on the Move: New Migration Flows in Europe*, Council of Europe Press, pp. 41–82.

Serow, W., Nam, C., Sly, D. and Robert, W. (1990), *Handbook on International Migration*, London: Greenwood Press.

Simon, J. (1989), *The Economic Consequences of Immigration*, Cambridge: Blackwell (in association with the Cato Institute).

Stark, O. (1991a), *The Migration of Labor*, Cambridge, Massachusetts: Blackwell, chapter 9.

Stark, O. (1991b), *The Migration of Labor*, Cambridge, Massachusetts: Blackwell, chapter 13.

Straubhaar, T. and Zimmermann, K. (1992), 'Towards a European Migration Policy', CEPR Discussion Paper, No. 641.

Tirole, J. (1988), *The Theory of Industrial Organization*, Cambridge, Mass.: M.I.T. Press.

Tobin, J. and Buiter, W. (1976), 'Long Run Effects of Fiscal and Monetary Policy on Aggregate Demand' in Stein, J. (ed.), *Monetarism*, Amsterdam: North-Holland.

Turnovsky, S. (1986), 'Monetary and Fiscal Policy under Perfect Foresight: A Symmetric Two-Country Analysis', *Economica*, 53, pp. 139–57.

Uzawa, H. (1969), 'Time Preference and the Penrose Effect in a Two Class Model of Economic Growth', *Journal of Political Economy*, 77, pp. 628–52.

Van der Ploeg (1988), 'International Interdependence and Policy Coordination in Economies With Real and Nominal Wage Rigidity' in Courakis and Taylor (eds), *Private Behaviour and Government Policy in Interdependent Economies*, London: MacMillan Press.

Van der Ploeg (1995), 'International Interdependence and Macroeconomic Policy Coordination' in Pikoulakis, E. (ed.), *International Macroeconomics*, London: Macmillan Press.

Vijverberg, W.P. (1993), 'Labour Market Performance as a Determinant of Migration', *Economica*, 60, pp. 143–60.

Widgren, J. (1987), 'International Migration: New Challenges to Europe', report prepared for the Third Conference of European Ministers Responsible for Migration, organized by the Council of Europe, Porto, Portugal, 13–15 May.

Winkelmann, R. and Zimmerman, K. (1993), 'Ageing, Migration and Labour Mobility' in Jonhnson, P. and Zimmerman, K. (eds), *Labour Supply in An Ageing Europe*, Cambridge University Press.

Zervoyianni, A. (1988), 'Exchange Rate Overshooting, Currency Substitution and Monetary Policy', *The Manchester School*, 56, pp. 247–67.

Zervoyianni, A. (1992), 'International Macroeconomic Interdependence, Currency Substitution, and Price Stickiness', *Journal of Macroeconomics*, 14, pp. 59–86.

Zervoyianni, A. (1993), 'Insider-Outsider Conflicts and Monetary Policy Games in Interdependent Economies', *Dynamis, Quaderno*, 9/93, Istituto di Ricerca Sulla Dinamica dei Sistemi Economici, Milan.

Zimmerman, K. (1992), 'Industrial Restructuring, Unemployment and Migration' in Jackuemin, A. (ed.), *Europe and Economic Interdependence*, Cambridge: Cambridge University Press.